Commercial Property Millionaire Secrets

Table of Contents

Chapter 1 - Understanding Financing Options	1
Understanding Financing Options	1
Evaluating Different Loan Options	3
Forming Strategic Partnerships	10
Strategizing Financial Approaches for Optimal Outcomes	18
Chapter 2 - Value-Added Investment Strategies	22
Value-Added Investment Strategies	22
Identifying Undervalued Properties for Potential Growth	24
Implementing Renovation Projects to Increase Property Value	30
Leveraging Technology for Market Analysis and Enhancement	38
Exploring the Concept of Adaptive Reuse for Maximum Returns	46
Maximizing Returns through Strategic Value-Add Investments	53
Chapter 3 - Long-Term Wealth Building	56
Long-Term Wealth Building	56
Creating a Diversified Real Estate Portfolio for Stability	58
Understanding Market Cycles and Their Impact on Investments	63
Implementing Tax Strategies for Long-Term Financial Gains	69
Optimizing Property Management for Sustained Income Growth	75
Achieving Long-Term Prosperity Through Strategic Real Estate Investments	82
Chapter 4 - Market Analysis and Forecasting	86
Market Analysis and Forecasting	86
Understanding Economic Indicators Affecting Commercial Property Values	88
Implementing Predictive Analytics for Anticipating Market Trends	94

Assessing Demand-Supply Dynamics in Key Markets	100
Incorporating Competitive Analysis for Strategic Positioning	108
Strategic Approaches to Market Analysis and Forecasting	115
Chapter 5 - Financial Analysis Techniques	118
Financial Analysis Techniques	118
Understanding the Importance of Cash Flow Analysis	120
Learning How to Calculate ROI for Property Acquisitions	125
Exploring Risk Assessment Models for Project Evaluations	133
Mastering Budgeting and Forecasting Methods for Real Estate Ventures	139
Integrating Financial Analysis for Commercial Real Estate Success	147
Chapter 6 - Exit Strategies for Real Estate Investments	150
Exit Strategies for Real Estate Investments	150
Leveraging Sale-Leaseback Arrangements for Liquidity	152
Maximizing Tax Efficiency with 1031 Exchanges	159
Strategic Exits: Unlocking Value and Mitigating Risk	165

Chapter 1 - Understanding Financing Options

Understanding Financing Options

Navigating the labyrinth of financing options in commercial real estate can feel overwhelming, but understanding these pathways is crucial for making informed investment decisions. Whether you are a seasoned investor or a newcomer looking to diversify your portfolio, grasping the array of available financing mechanisms is essential. By demystifying loan types, ratios, and alternative funding sources, this chapter aims to equip you with the knowledge needed to secure profitable deals while mitigating financial risks.

One of the primary challenges investors face is selecting the most suitable loan option from a multitude of choices, each with its unique benefits and limitations. For instance, conventional mortgages offer predictable terms and are favored by established businesses with solid cash flows. However, they may not be ideal for small businesses or startups due to their stringent eligibility criteria. Alternatively, SBA loans cater specifically to smaller enterprises with more accessible terms but come with extensive documentation requirements. Another critical aspect is understanding key financial metrics such as the loan-to-value (LTV) ratio and the debt service coverage ratio (DSCR), which help evaluate a loan's feasibility. A lower LTV ratio generally indicates reduced risk and can lead to better loan conditions, while a higher DSCR suggests that an investment property can comfortably cover its debt obligations.

This chapter delves into various financing avenues, offering a comprehensive guide on evaluating different loan types, including conventional mortgages and SBA loans, and understanding crucial financial ratios. Moreover, it explores alternative funding sources like private lenders and hard money loans, which provide flexibility at a higher cost. The chapter also discusses the importance of loan amortization schedules and prepayment penalties, ensuring you are well-informed about long-term financial commitments. By the end of this chapter, you will have a robust framework for assessing and choosing the best financing options tailored to your specific investment needs.

Evaluating Different Loan Options

Understanding the implications of various loan options in commercial real estate financing is paramount for any savvy investor looking to expand their wealth through strategic property acquisitions. Different types of loans, such as conventional mortgages or SBA loans, offer varying interest rates and terms that can significantly impact your investment returns.

Conventional mortgages are often the go-to for many seasoned investors due to their straightforward nature. They typically feature fixed or variable interest rates and longer repayment terms, making them ideal for well-established businesses with consistent cash flows. On the other hand, SBA loans, like the SBA 7(a) and SBA 504 programs, cater primarily to small businesses. The SBA 504 loan, for example, provides a fixed-rate option aimed explicitly at major fixed assets like real estate (Alloy Development Co., 2023). Smaller upfront costs and favorable terms can make SBA loans attractive, but they come with stringent eligibility criteria and extensive documentation requirements.

Now, grasping the concepts of loan-to-value (LTV) ratios and debt service coverage ratios (DSCR) is crucial for assessing the feasibility of these financing options. The LTV ratio measures the loan amount against the market value of the property. A lower LTV ratio generally indicates less risk for the lender and can result in more favorable loan terms for you, the borrower. To navigate this effectively:

- First, determine the appraised market value of the property.
- Then, calculate the maximum loan amount you can afford while maintaining an acceptable LTV ratio.
- Ensure that your down payment covers enough of the property's value to keep the LTV ratio within a manageable range.

Evaluating the DSCR is equally important. This ratio compares a property's annual net operating income to its annual mortgage debt service. A higher DSCR suggests that the property generates sufficient income to cover debt payments, which not only reassures lenders but also provides peace of mind that the investment is sound. Here's a guideline approach:

- Calculate the net operating income (NOI) by subtracting operating expenses from total revenue.

- Divide the NOI by the annual debt service to get your DSCR.
- Aim for a DSCR above 1.2 to ensure some buffer against income fluctuations.

Exploring alternative financing sources, such as private lenders or hard money loans, can offer flexibility but often at a higher cost. Private lenders might be more willing to take on risk compared to traditional banks, and they may provide faster approvals with less paperwork. However, this ease comes with steeper interest rates and shorter repayment periods. Hard money loans, secured by the property's value rather than the borrower's creditworthiness, appeal to those needing quick funding or unconventional properties. Still, they demand careful consideration. To navigate these alternatives:

- Assess the loan's total cost, considering both interest rates and additional fees.

- Evaluate the repayment timeline and ensure it aligns with your investment strategy.
- Prepare for higher down payments and have a clear exit strategy to manage higher financial risks.

Loan amortization schedules and prepayment penalties are additional facets to understand to make informed decisions about your financing strategies. Amortization schedules show how loan payments are applied towards interest and principal over time, with early payments typically covering more interest than principal. Understanding this can help you forecast long-term costs and manage cash flow efficiently. Furthermore, prepayment penalties—fees charged for paying off a loan ahead of schedule—can sometimes negate the benefits of early repayment. Here's how you can stay on top of these factors:

- Review the loan amortization schedule provided by your lender

to understand the breakdown of payments over time.
- Factor in the impact of prepayment penalties when considering refinancing or early payoff.
- Regularly assess your investment's performance to decide whether accelerating loan payments aligns with your financial goals.

Incorporating these insights can greatly enhance your ability to evaluate and select the best commercial real estate financing options. By leveraging empirical data and thorough research, you can balance economic growth and personal welfare, ensuring that every investment decision not only supports your individual freedom but also contributes positively to society. Robust evidence backs the need for reforms that empower people with greater control over their financial destinies, reinforcing the importance of social responsibility alongside personal gain.

Consider the broader landscape: While governments and corporations possess the resources to influence markets significantly, it's essential to advocate for a system where checks and balances protect public interests. Collaborative efforts between public and private sectors can foster environments where economic growth dovetails neatly with improved human welfare. For instance, measures like the SBA's community support initiatives and regional development programs highlight the potential for synergistic partnerships (Alloy Development Co., 2023).

Taking a comprehensive view of financing options in commercial real estate doesn't just impact your bottom line; it positions you to contribute to a more balanced, responsible economy. In today's polarized political climate, championing evidence-driven policies that address personal concerns while promoting collective well-being is paramount. Empowerment through knowledge and meticulous planning can lead to smarter investments that benefit both individuals and the broader community.

By mastering the intricacies of loan types, leveraging appropriate ratios for financial assessment, exploring flexible yet costly alternatives, and understanding the nuances of loan amortization, you equip yourself with the tools needed for successful commercial real estate ventures. Remember, each financing decision holds the potential to build not only personal wealth but also a sustainable, equitable future for all stakeholders involved.

Forming Strategic Partnerships

Exploring partnerships as a viable financing strategy in commercial real estate investments is an intelligent approach to accessing additional capital and expertise, securing larger deals, and sharing financial risks. Engaging with experienced investors or real estate professionals can open doors to opportunities that might otherwise be out of reach.

Partnering with investors or real estate professionals can provide access to additional capital and expertise to secure larger deals. This means you are not bearing the financial burden alone, and you benefit from the combined knowledge and experience of your partners. Here's how to navigate this:

- Identify potential investors or real estate professionals who have a track record of successful projects. Look for those who bring not just money but also valuable insight into the market.
- Approach these potential partners with a well-prepared business plan that outlines the project details, potential returns, and the specific role you envision for them. This will demonstrate your professionalism and increase their confidence in collaborating with you.
- Communicate clearly your goals, timelines, and expectations to

ensure everyone is on the same page from the outset. Transparency is key in building trust and fostering a productive partnership.

Collaborating with equity partners or syndicates can spread financial risks and leverage combined resources for profitable ventures. Though it might sound complex, the essence is relatively straightforward. When multiple parties pool their resources, the risk inherent in any single investment is diluted. Each party's exposure is minimized, making it easier to weather challenges and capitalize on successes.

However, establishing clear partnership agreements outlining roles, responsibilities, and profit-sharing arrangements is essential for successful collaboration. Without question, clarity in these agreements will be the backbone of your partnership's success.

- Start by drafting a detailed agreement that lays out each

partner's contribution concerning capital, expertise, and responsibilities. This document should be clear and comprehensive, leaving no room for ambiguity.

- Define the profit-sharing structure explicitly. Who gets what, when, and under what conditions? These details prevent future misunderstandings and conflicts.
- Establish mechanisms for decision-making within the partnership. Determine upfront how decisions will be made, whether through a majority vote, unanimous consent, or some other method.
- Include clear exit strategies in your agreement. Real estate investments can span many years, so it's critical to know how partners can leave the venture or dissolve the partnership if necessary.

Leveraging networking opportunities and industry connections can help in identifying suitable partners for diverse real estate projects. The power of networking cannot be overstated—it's often through relationships and connections that the best opportunities arise.

- Attend industry events like conferences, seminars, and workshops where you can meet potential partners face-to-face. Personal interaction often leads to more meaningful connections than digital communication alone.

- Join professional associations related to real estate. Being part of organizations provides regular opportunities to interact with likeminded professionals and keep abreast of industry trends.

- Utilize online platforms dedicated to real estate investments and networking. Websites like LinkedIn can be powerful tools for finding and connecting with people who share your investment interests.

- Engage in community activities and forums where local real estate professionals gather. Building a reputation as a knowledgeable and trustworthy individual in your community can attract potential partners to you.

Now let's consider the broader implications of these strategies. Utilizing partnerships effectively taps into a wide range of possibilities that single-handed endeavors can't match. Pooling resources not only amplifies financial capacity but also enhances strategic insights. Recognizing and aligning with partners who hold complementary strengths will make your ventures robust against market volatilities.

Moreover, evidence suggests joint-venture strategies are gaining popularity worldwide among investors looking for new market entries and portfolio diversification. According to a 2021 report by NAIOP, joint-ventures are increasingly common in the U.S., particularly in office acquisitions. They allow for diversified risk and closer alignment of interests between partners (Why Investors Are Homing in on Joint Venture Strategies, 2021).

Such arrangements are typically structured with general and limited partners. The general partner operates or manages the venture while the limited partner provides most of the required equity capital, ensuring alignment of interests. By sharing risks and responsibilities, both parties stand to gain significantly from the resulting synergy (Wharton Executive Education, 2024).

As we delve deeper into these partnerships, it's worth noting that the choice of partners and the nature of agreements play crucial roles. Not all partnerships are created equal, nor do they guarantee success absent clear agreements and mutual understanding.

Empirical data further supports these insights. Research from Wharton's executive education programs indicates that understanding various sectors within commercial real estate, analyzing short- and long-term trends, and balancing risks and returns are critical components for successful investment (Wharton Executive Education, 2024). When selecting partners, it's imperative to evaluate their compatibility with your investment horizon and risk tolerance to avoid potential conflicts.

To summarize, the benefits of leveraging partnerships in commercial real estate investments are multifaceted. The infusion of extra capital and expertise enables you to take on larger, more lucrative projects. Collaborating spreads financial risk, making ventures safer and more appealing. Detailed partnership agreements ensure smooth operations and mitigate disputes, while robust networking fosters advantageous connections. By strategically implementing these guidelines, you're well-positioned to maximize your returns and create sustainable, profitable investments.

Embarking on these steps could revolutionize your approach to commercial real estate, propelling you toward greater achievements and financial stability. Consider partnerships not just as a funding mechanism, but as a pathway to innovation, resilience, and ultimately, success in the complex yet rewarding realm of commercial real estate.

Strategizing Financial Approaches for Optimal Outcomes

In this chapter, we have navigated through the landscape of financing options available for commercial real estate investments. From conventional mortgages known for their straightforward nature to SBA loans that cater to small businesses with favorable terms and stringent requirements, we've dissected each option's nuances. Additionally, understanding key financial ratios like LTV and DSCR has equipped us to evaluate the feasibility and soundness of these financing choices thoroughly.

We also delved into alternative sources such as private lenders and hard money loans, evaluating their pros and cons against traditional banking routes. While these options offer flexibility and quicker approvals, they come with higher interest rates and greater financial risks, necessitating careful cost assessment and strategic planning.

Furthermore, we explored how loan amortization schedules and prepayment penalties can influence long-term costs and repayment strategies. By mastering these aspects, you can better forecast expenses and manage your cash flow efficiently, ensuring that your investment decisions are not only informed but also prudent.

Returning to our initial assertion regarding the importance of understanding various financing options, it is evident that leveraging empirical data and thorough research is crucial. The integration of knowledge concerning loan types, financial ratios, and alternative funding mechanisms provides a robust foundation for making educated investment decisions. This solid footing enables you to balance economic growth with personal welfare, thus fostering a socially responsible approach to wealth accumulation.

For some readers, the complexity of navigating these financial waters might be concerning. However, the consequences of well-informed decisions in commercial real estate are far-reaching. Not only do these choices impact personal financial health, but they also hold the potential to contribute positively to broader economic stability and community well-being.

Ultimately, employing a comprehensive view of financing strategies elevates your ability to make smarter investments, leading to a more equitable future. Each financing decision is a step towards building personal wealth while also supporting a balanced economy where collective prosperity is possible. As we conclude, consider your next move carefully. Reflect on how these insights can shape your investments and contribute to a sustainable, profitable future in commercial real estate.

Chapter 2 - Value-Added Investment Strategies

Value-Added Investment Strategies

In the ever-evolving landscape of commercial real estate, finding the right opportunities to invest can mean the difference between success and stagnation. The allure of discovering undervalued properties that hold the promise of significant appreciation is a key driver for many investors. Understanding how to identify these hidden gems and capitalize on them through value-added investment strategies is not just an art; it's a science informed by data, market trends, and strategic planning.

One of the primary challenges in commercial real estate investing is accurately identifying properties with untapped potential. Market indicators such as employment rates, population growth, and infrastructural developments play pivotal roles in revealing areas ripe for investment. For example, a neighborhood experiencing a surge in business expansions coupled with declining vacancy rates could indicate a rising demand for commercial space. However, simply recognizing these indicators isn't enough. Investors must conduct thorough due diligence, assessing everything from structural integrity to zoning compliance, to mitigate risks and accurately gauge a property's true value.

In this chapter, we will delve into several critical aspects of value-added investment strategies. You will learn how to analyze market indicators to single out undervalued properties poised for growth and discover effective methods for conducting comprehensive property inspections and due diligence. We'll also explore the nuances of negotiating favorable purchase terms and developing tactical marketing plans to attract buyers or tenants post-renovation. Through this guided approach, you will be equipped with practical tools and insights to maximize your returns and make informed, evidence-driven investment decisions in the competitive world of commercial real estate.

Identifying Undervalued Properties for Potential Growth

Understanding market indicators to identify undervalued properties and potential growth opportunities is a cornerstone of successful commercial real estate investing. Market indicators are like the pulse of the property world—they reveal the health, potential, and hidden gems within a given area. By analyzing these indicators, you can uncover undervalued properties poised for appreciation.

Economic data, such as employment rates, population growth, and business expansions, can provide insights into an area's vitality and future demand for commercial space. Pay attention to trends in rental yields and vacancy rates; declining vacancy rates coupled with steady or increasing rental yields often signal a burgeoning market ripe for investment. Additionally, infrastructure developments—like new transport links or business districts—can dramatically alter property values, acting as a catalyst for future growth. Always keep your ear to the ground and stay informed about planned projects and policy changes that might affect your target area.

Next, conducting thorough property inspections and due diligence is non-negotiable when assessing value-add potential. This involves more than just visiting the property; it's about diving deep into its physical and legal aspects to understand its true condition and any hidden risks. Here is what you can do in order to achieve the goal:

- First, start with a detailed inspection focusing on the structural integrity of the building. Look for signs of deferred maintenance or needed repairs, which could either be a negotiation point or a red flag.
- Second, evaluate the property's compliance with local zoning laws and regulations. Check for any

existing violations or required permits for potential renovations.

- Third, assess the potential for modern upgrades that could increase the property's appeal and functionality. Consider sustainability features like energy-efficient lighting or eco-friendly materials that might attract tenants who value green buildings.
- Fourth, dive into the financial records, including past rent rolls, operating expenses, and profit statements. Ensure accuracy by cross-referencing with third-party sources or employing a professional auditor.

Solid due diligence not only helps assess the current value but also forecasts future profitability scenarios, guiding you toward informed investment decisions.

Negotiating favorable purchase terms is another critical step. This process starts even before the initial offer, as preparation lays the groundwork for successful negotiation. Knowing the seller's motivations can give you leverage. If they're eager to sell quickly, you might secure a lower price or more flexible terms. Conversely, a seller who's in no hurry may require you to offer additional incentives.

Here's how to master this complex dance:

- First, arm yourself with a robust understanding of comparable sales in the area. Presenting factual data during negotiations can validate your offer price and help justify why it should be accepted.
- Second, consider incorporating creative financing options. These could include seller financing, where the seller allows you to pay over time, or lease-to-own arrangements, reducing the upfront capital required.
- Third, always have a backup plan. Whether it's a willingness to walk away or alternative properties lined

up, having options reduces the pressure on you to settle for unfavorable terms.

- Fourth, incorporate contingencies in your contract. These may include clauses allowing for further inspections or financing approval periods, providing you with exit points if unforeseen issues arise.

Effective negotiation ensures that you acquire the property at the best possible terms, maximizing your return on investment from the outset.

Implementing strategic marketing tactics to attract potential buyers or tenants post-renovation is the final piece of the puzzle. Once you've enhanced the property, it's time to showcase its value to the right audience. Your marketing strategy should be multi-faceted and targeted, highlighting the upgrades and benefits your property offers.

Consider these steps:

- Develop a strong online presence through high-quality photos, virtual tours, and detailed descriptions on major real estate platforms and social media channels.

- Highlight unique selling points, such as proximity to key landmarks, transport links, or the integration of smart technology and sustainable features.
- Create compelling content that tells a story about the property's transformation, potentially attracting media coverage and generating buzz.
- Utilize targeted advertising, focusing on demographics most likely to be interested in your property. This could mean promoting to businesses in growth sectors or targeting specific tenant types, like tech startups or retail franchises.

Proper research and analysis are instrumental in identifying undervalued properties, while adept negotiating skills can significantly boost profit margins. Remember, it's not just about finding a good deal but also about transforming that deal into a lucrative asset through careful planning, execution, and marketing. Balancing economic growth with human welfare ensures your investments benefit not just your portfolio but also the community they serve.

By following these strategies, investors can navigate the complexities of commercial real estate to uncover and capitalize on value-added opportunities. Consistent effort and an evidence-driven approach will yield fruitful returns, making your journey through the commercial real estate landscape both rewarding and impactful.

Implementing Renovation Projects to Increase Property Value

Utilizing cost-effective renovation strategies to enhance property aesthetics and functionality involves a delicate balance between creativity and practical-minded planning. As an evidence-driven individual, I find it crucial to rely not just on intuition but solid data to make these decisions. Researching current market trends and tenant preferences serves as the foundation, helping guide which renovation projects will yield the highest return on investment. For instance, incorporating open floor plans or modern lighting can significantly elevate the property's allure without breaking the bank.

Here is what you can do in order to achieve the goal:

- First, consult recent studies or reports on what features are in high demand in your local market.
- Second, focus on cosmetic updates such as fresh paint, new fixtures, and landscaping – these changes are often less expensive but can dramatically improve the property's appearance.
- Third, opt for materials that offer a good balance between cost and durability. Think laminate flooring that mimics hardwood or quartz

countertops instead of more expensive granite.

- Fourth, always get multiple quotes for renovation work to ensure you're getting competitive pricing. Comparing costs will help you maximize every dollar spent.

The collaboration with skilled contractors and architects is another pivot point in executing renovation projects efficiently. I've found that establishing relationships with professionals who share your vision and understand the importance of both time and budget constraints is paramount. Good rapport leads to smoother project execution, fewer misunderstandings, and ultimately better results. Start by vetting potential collaborators thoroughly. Check their references, review their past work, and gauge their responsiveness and willingness to accommodate your needs.

Here is what you can do in order to achieve the goal:
- First, interview multiple contractors and architects to find those who best align with your project's vision and objectives.
- Second, clearly outline your expectations, timelines, and budget constraints upfront to avoid any future misunderstandings.
- Third, maintain open lines of communication throughout the project. Regular meetings and updates can preempt potential issues and keep everyone on the same page.
- Fourth, don't hesitate to ask for progress reports and visit the site frequently to ensure work is proceeding according to plan.

Incorporating sustainable and energy-efficient features is not just an altruistic move; it's a smart business strategy that meets the growing demand for green buildings. Tenants and buyers are increasingly looking for properties that reflect their environmental values, and having these features can set your property apart from the competition. Start by conducting a thorough energy audit to identify key areas where improvements can be made. Solar panels, energy-efficient lighting, and high-performance insulation are some initial steps that can dramatically reduce utility bills and attract eco-conscious tenants.

Here is what you can do in order to achieve the goal:

- First, conduct an energy audit to identify key areas that need improvement.
- Second, prioritize high-impact, low-cost upgrades like energy-efficient lighting and smart thermostats.
- Third, consider larger investments like solar panels or upgrading HVAC systems for long-term savings.

- Fourth, make sure to highlight these green features in your marketing materials to attract environmentally conscious tenants or buyers.

Monitoring renovation progress and budgeting closely is where the rubber meets the road. This is where all the planning and careful selection of partners pays off – or doesn't, if you're not vigilant. Staying on top of the project timeline and expenses ensures that your renovations don't spiral out of control, eroding the potential value they were intended to add. Use project management tools or software to track progress in real-time, and establish clear milestones that must be met before moving on to the next phase. Frequent site visits are indispensable in this regard, offering a firsthand look at the pace of work and any emerging issues.

Here is what you can do in order to achieve the goal:
- First, use project management tools to create a detailed renovation timeline with clear milestones.
- Second, establish a regular schedule for site visits to oversee the progress personally.
- Third, maintain a close eye on expenditures to ensure you stay within budget, using software or spreadsheets to track every cost.
- Fourth, have contingency plans in place for unexpected delays or expenses. These can include setting aside a portion of your budget for unforeseen issues.

Aligning renovations with market trends and tenant preferences is vital to ensuring the long-term success of your investment. By focusing on what the market wants, you increase the likelihood of higher occupancy rates and returns. Conduct surveys or focus groups if possible, to gather direct feedback from potential tenants. This empirical approach provides the insights needed to tailor your renovations to what people are genuinely looking for, rather than relying on assumptions.

Sustainability considerations, as mentioned, can have a powerful impact on attracting premium tenants and adding value. Sustainable building practices are not just a trend; they're becoming a standard. Properties with LEED certifications or similar credentials tend to command higher rents and retain tenants longer. The financial benefits of lower utility costs and the reduced environmental footprint create win-win situations for both landlords and tenants.

In conclusion, implementing effective renovation projects to increase property value requires a multi-faceted approach. Utilizing cost-effective strategies, collaborating with skilled professionals, incorporating sustainable features, and monitoring progress meticulously are each critical components. Remember, renovations should always align with current market demands and preferences to maximize their impact. Balancing economic growth with human welfare, particularly through thoughtful and empirically-informed choices, promises not just financial gains but also societal benefits, echoing the broader principles of personal responsibility fused with social consciousness.

Leveraging Technology for Market Analysis and Enhancement

Leveraging technology in real estate investment isn't just about staying current; it's about enhancing efficiency and ensuring that investment decisions are as informed as possible. To achieve this, the inclusion of innovative tools and data-driven strategies is essential.

Let's start by discussing how real estate software can revolutionize market analysis and property valuation. This kind of software offers comprehensive insights that would be challenging, if not impossible, to obtain manually. By consolidating a plethora of data points—such as market trends, historical property values, neighborhood statistics, and even macroeconomic factors—these platforms provide a nuanced understanding of what makes an investment worthwhile. Here's what you can do to leverage such tools effectively:

- Firstly, identify a trusted real estate software platform with robust analytic capabilities. Make sure it aligns well with your specific investment goals.
- Once you've selected a platform, familiarize yourself with its interface and functionalities. Take full advantage of training resources or tutorials often provided by the software developers.
- Use the software to gather and analyze data from various sources. This will help produce a comprehensive market analysis report, enabling you to make more

accurate valuations and informed decisions.

- Finally, frequently update your data inputs and continuously monitor the market climate through the software. Staying updated ensures your analyses remain relevant and timely.

Next, let's delve into the realm of digital marketing—a powerful strategy for showcasing value-added properties. Traditional marketing methods still hold value, but a robust online presence has become indispensable in today's fast-paced digital world. To reach a broader audience and highlight the unique advantages of your commercial properties, consider implementing these simple yet effective guidelines:

- Develop a dynamic and user-friendly website showcasing your portfolio of properties. Include high-quality images, virtual tours, detailed descriptions, and any value-added features that distinguish your properties from competitors.

- Utilize social media platforms to engage with potential clients and investors. Platforms like LinkedIn, Instagram, and Facebook offer targeted advertising options to reach your desired demographic.
- Invest in search engine optimization (SEO) to ensure your properties appear in relevant searches. Well-crafted content that incorporates strategic keywords can significantly improve visibility.
- Establish an email marketing campaign to keep interested parties updated on new listings, open houses, and special events. Personalized email campaigns can foster stronger client relationships and enhance engagement.

Transitioning from marketing to property management brings us to the concept of integrating smart building technologies. These innovations are pivotal in elevating property management efficiency and tenant satisfaction. Smart tech includes everything from energy-efficient lighting systems to advanced security protocols, all designed to streamline operations and enhance tenant experiences. Here's how you can start integrating these technologies:

- Begin by assessing the current technological framework of your properties. Identify areas where smart upgrades could yield significant improvements in efficiency or tenant satisfaction.
- Integrate smart thermostats and HVAC systems to optimize energy consumption. Not only does this lower operational costs, but it also appeals to environmentally conscious tenants.
- Implement smart security systems, including surveillance cameras and access control features. Enhanced security measures can provide peace of mind to both tenants and property managers.

- Consider adopting tenant management apps that allow residents to submit maintenance requests, pay rent, and communicate with management seamlessly. A smooth and responsive management experience can greatly improve tenant retention rates.

Lastly, adopting data-driven decision-making processes is vital for optimizing investment returns and overall property performance. In an era where data is king, leveraging this wealth of information can make all the difference between a good investment and a great one. Follow these steps to harness the power of data in your investment strategy:

- Collect data from diverse sources, including financial reports, market analytics, tenant feedback, and industry benchmarks. The more comprehensive your data pool, the more precise your insights will be.

- Employ data visualization tools to transform raw data into comprehensible charts and graphs. Visual representations can reveal patterns, trends, and correlations that might not be immediately apparent from spreadsheets alone.
- Utilize predictive analytics to forecast future market conditions, rental income potentials, and property values. Predictive models can guide you in making proactive rather than reactive decisions.
- Regularly review and refine your data strategies. As new data becomes available and market conditions evolve, continuous improvement ensures your decision-making process remains cutting-edge.

By utilizing real estate software, implementing digital marketing strategies, integrating smart building technologies, and adopting data-driven decision-making processes, you're setting yourself up for success in commercial real estate investing. Technology can indeed streamline investment processes and significantly enhance property performance. It is vital to remember that while economic growth is important, human welfare should always take precedence in your investment decisions. Balancing these aspects will not only drive better returns but also contribute to a more sustainable and equitable market landscape.

In conclusion, embracing technology in the realm of commercial real estate isn't merely about keeping pace with advancements. It's about unlocking new levels of efficiency, reaching wider audiences, enhancing tenant satisfaction, and making more informed investment choices. By integrating these strategies thoughtfully and systematically, you can navigate the complexities of the commercial real estate market and build a resilient, prosperous portfolio.

Exploring the Concept of Adaptive Reuse for Maximum Returns

Let's dive right in and explore how repurposing existing properties to meet current market demands can be a goldmine for commercial real estate investors. The concept of adaptive reuse involves transforming old structures into something new and functional, providing immense value not just financially but also socially. Imagine converting a dated factory building into trendy loft apartments or turning an abandoned warehouse into a bustling marketplace. These projects offer incredible opportunities for value-added investments where creativity meets practicality.

Here is what you can do in order to achieve the goal:

- First, identify buildings that have fallen out of use but are located in areas with rising demand.
- Next, assess the structural integrity and potential for modification.
- Then, study the local market trends to determine what types of facilities

are in scarcity—be it residential units, office spaces, or retail outlets.
- Finally, develop a plan that harmonizes the existing structure with the new intended use, whether through minor renovations or major overhauls.

Understanding zoning regulations and environmental considerations plays a crucial role in any adaptive reuse project. Zoning laws dictate how you can use a property and understanding these rules early on can save time and money. Environmental concerns such as contamination of the site or the sustainable use of resources also come into play. For instance, some older buildings may require extensive clean-up before they can be repurposed. While this might seem daunting, it's essential to factor these elements into your planning process.

Zoning restrictions can sometimes feel like a maze, but with careful navigation, they're manageable. Before diving in, make sure you fully understand the zoning codes in the area. Consult with local zoning officials or hire experts who can guide you through the regulatory requirements. Often, zoning laws will specify what types of developments are permissible in a given area, so it's vital to ensure that your vision aligns with these guidelines. This preparation stage can prevent costly delays or legal hurdles down the line.

Next, consider leveraging the historical or architectural value inherent in many older structures. Buildings from different eras often have unique features that modern constructions lack—think ornate facades, high ceilings, or intricate woodwork. These elements can attract niche markets, like history aficionados or businesses looking for a distinctive space. By preserving and highlighting these architectural gems, you add cultural and aesthetic value, making your property stand out in a crowded market.

Here is what you can do in order to achieve the goal:

- Identify historical elements worth preserving.
- Partner with historians or architects specializing in historical renovations.
- Incorporate these elements into your design plans to retain authenticity.
- Promote these unique features during marketing to attract niche buyers or tenants.

Engaging with community stakeholders and local authorities is another critical component when pursuing adaptive reuse initiatives. These groups can significantly influence your project's success or failure. Community members often have strong opinions about local development, and gaining their support can smooth the approval process. Attend community meetings and listen to concerns and needs; this will help build positive relationships and foster goodwill.

Local authorities can provide valuable insights and support, especially if your project aligns with broader community or city development goals. For example, cities increasingly prioritize sustainable development, and an adaptive reuse project can serve as a model for combining growth with ecological responsibility. Collaborating with these entities ensures your project meets regulatory standards and garners public support.

Here is what you can do to gain community and authority support:

- Initiate dialogues with local leaders and community members to understand their concerns and aspirations.
- Foster transparency by sharing your vision and detailed plans for the project.

- Seek endorsements from influential community members or groups.
- Address any environmental or social impacts proactively to demonstrate your commitment to responsible development.

Adaptive reuse projects present a win-win scenario: they can generate significant returns while contributing positively to community sustainability. Instead of erecting new structures that consume more resources and disrupt existing neighborhoods, adaptive reuse breathes new life into dormant spaces. It cuts down on waste and carbon footprints, aligning well with growing environmental awareness among investors and consumers alike.

Comprehensive planning and stakeholder engagement are fundamental to the success of these ventures. A well-thought-out strategy that considers market demands, zoning laws, historical value, and community input is far more likely to succeed than one that overlooks these factors. Each adaptive reuse project, though complex, offers a rewarding pathway to creating value out of disuse, blending economic growth with enhanced human welfare.

Remember, the key takeaways here are simple yet powerful: adaptive reuse projects can turn overlooked properties into profitable investments while fostering sustainable community growth. But to navigate successfully, you'll need comprehensive planning and active engagement with all stakeholders involved. With these strategies in place, you're well on your way to unlocking hidden value in commercial real estate.

By championing adaptive reuse, we can achieve a delicate balance between personal financial growth and societal good. It allows us to invest wisely while considering the long-term impact on our communities and environment. So, fellow investors, let's embrace the challenge of revitalizing our urban landscapes thoughtfully and responsibly, securing both financial rewards and a brighter future for all.

Maximizing Returns through Strategic Value-Add Investments

In this chapter, we've delved into the myriad opportunities and strategic approaches that can enhance your investment endeavors in commercial real estate. By identifying undervalued properties and potential growth markets through diligent analysis of market indicators, including economic data, rental yields, vacancy rates, and infrastructure developments, investors can uncover hidden gems ripe for profitable transformation.

Reflecting on the introduction's emphasis on understanding market dynamics, it's clear that thorough due diligence is paramount. This examination isn't limited to property inspections; it also extends to legal compliances, financial records, and potential for modern upgrades. Each step—from assessing structural integrity to scrutinizing zoning laws—lays a foundation for informed decision-making.

A sound negotiating strategy ensures favorable purchase terms, starting with grasping the seller's motivations and using comparable sales data effectively. Incorporating creative financing and maintaining contingency plans further provide an edge during these critical negotiations.

Marketing renovated properties demands a solid strategy, focusing on multifaceted and targeted efforts. Emphasizing unique selling points, leveraging online platforms, and telling engaging stories about the property's transformation can attract the right buyers or tenants.

Concerns may arise regarding the potential risks involved, such as misjudging market trends or underestimating renovation costs. Due diligence mitigates these risks, but remaining vigilant and adaptable is crucial.

Wider implications of your investments also resonate. Beyond individual gains, strategic investments can rejuvenate communities, contributing to local economic growth and improving societal welfare.

As we conclude, remember that the journey in commercial real estate is continuous and evolving. Stay committed to consistent effort, evidence-driven decisions, and a balanced approach. The landscape may shift, but the principles of thorough research, strategic negotiation, and adaptive marketing remain steadfast. With these tools, you can navigate and capitalize on the ever-changing terrain of commercial real estate, creating not just wealth but lasting value for the community and beyond.

Chapter 3 - Long-Term Wealth Building

Long-Term Wealth Building

Building long-term wealth through commercial real estate requires more than just intuition—it demands a well-thought-out strategy. Imagine navigating the complex world of investments without a map; it would be easy to lose direction. In the realm of real estate, creating and maintaining a diversified portfolio serves as that essential map, guiding you toward consistent returns while cushioning against unpredictable market shifts.

One significant challenge investors face is the volatility inherent in any investment market, including commercial real estate. Market fluctuations can drastically affect the value of properties and rental incomes. For example, an economic downturn may hit retail spaces hard, causing vacancies and lower rents, while industrial warehouses might remain stable or even see increased demand.

By spreading investments across different property types—such as office buildings, retail spaces, industrial properties, and multifamily residences—you reduce the risk of experiencing substantial losses from a single market segment. This diversification acts as a safety net, ensuring that not all areas of your portfolio are impacted simultaneously by adverse conditions.

In this chapter, we will explore various strategies for building a robust real estate portfolio aimed at long-term wealth accumulation. We will delve into the importance of diversification and how it helps mitigate risks associated with market cycles. You'll learn how to balance high-risk, high-return investments with safer, more stable options effectively. Additionally, we'll discuss how to identify suitable property types and locations, monitor your investments over time, and adjust your portfolio in response to changing market dynamics. By the end of this chapter, you'll have a comprehensive understanding of how to craft a resilient portfolio that stands the test of time, guiding you toward sustained financial growth.

Creating a Diversified Real Estate Portfolio for Stability

Diversifying your real estate portfolio is one of the most effective ways to achieve long-term wealth accumulation while minimizing risks. By spreading investments across various property types and locations, you not only safeguard against market fluctuations but also place yourself in a stronger position to reap consistent and reliable returns over time.

First, let's talk about why diversification is crucial. Market fluctuations are an inherent part of any investment landscape, and commercial real estate is no different. By diversifying, you mitigate the risk that comes from having all your eggs in one basket. If one sector or geographic area experiences a downturn, other segments of your portfolio can remain unaffected or even thrive, providing a cushion against losses. For instance, an economic slump might impact retail spaces but leave industrial properties relatively untouched. This balance is invaluable for maintaining portfolio stability.

Furthermore, diversification enables investors to take advantage of various market cycles. Markets cycle through phases of growth, peak, recession, and recovery at different times and rates. By having a mix of property types and locations, you can benefit from these cycles more effectively. When office spaces in metropolitan areas hit a peak, suburban residential properties might just be entering a growth phase. The key lies in identifying and leveraging these cyclical opportunities to optimize your returns. It's about playing the long game and staying agile by adapting to an ever-changing market environment.

Now, let's delve into the unique income streams and growth potentials offered by different property types.

Commercial real estate isn't a monolith; it encompasses everything from office buildings and retail spaces to industrial warehouses and multifamily residences. Each type comes with its own set of advantages and challenges. Office buildings generally offer higher rental incomes but might suffer during economic downturns when businesses downsize. Retail spaces can be lucrative, especially if located in high-traffic areas, but require careful tenant selection to avoid vacancies. Industrial properties often have long-term tenants, providing stable income, but may be geographically limited. Multifamily residences, on the other hand, offer steady cash flow and tend to be more resilient during economic downturns as housing remains a necessity. Diversifying into these various property types ensures a steady and stable income stream, fortifying your portfolio against unexpected market shifts.

Balancing risk and return is another critical aspect of sustained wealth building in commercial real estate. While high-risk investments offer the potential for higher returns, they also come with greater uncertainty. Conversely, low-risk investments provide stability but might yield lower returns. An effective strategy involves blending these varying risk levels to achieve a balanced portfolio. This means occasionally taking calculated risks on high-growth potential properties while ensuring that a significant portion of your holdings remains in safer, more predictable investments. Striking this balance requires continual monitoring and reassessment of your portfolio to ensure it aligns with your long-term financial goals.

Understanding the benefits of diversification is just the start. Identifying suitable property types for a balanced portfolio demands detailed research and a deep understanding of market dynamics. You need to assess factors like location, economic indicators, tenant quality, and property condition. Think of it as putting together a puzzle where each piece plays a crucial role in forming the big picture.

Monitoring and adjusting your mix over time is equally important. Real estate markets are dynamic, and what works today may not work tomorrow. Regularly reviewing your investments ensures that your portfolio remains aligned with current market trends and your personal financial objectives. This might mean selling off underperforming assets or capitalizing on emerging market opportunities. The goal is to stay flexible and responsive to changes, continuously optimizing your investment strategy.

In conclusion, creating a diversified real estate portfolio is pivotal for achieving long-term wealth accumulation. It reduces risk, allows you to leverage different market cycles, introduces multiple income streams, and balances risk with return. By understanding these principles and applying them diligently, you're well on your way to building a robust and resilient portfolio that stands the test of time. Remember, the road to financial freedom through real estate isn't a sprint—it's a marathon. Stay informed, stay diversified, and most importantly, stay committed to your long-term goals.

Understanding Market Cycles and Their Impact on Investments

Recognizing the stages of market cycles is foundational to successful commercial real estate investment. Market cycles typically consist of various phases: growth, peak, decline, and recovery. By understanding these stages, investors can better anticipate trends and make informed decisions.

To illustrate, consider the growth phase, where the demand for properties often exceeds supply, leading to increasing rental rates and property values. This stage offers lucrative opportunities for acquisitions. Conversely, during the decline phase, an oversupply of properties forces rental rates down, and vacancies rise, which might be the ideal time to buy distressed properties at lower prices.

Now, looking at the strategic timing of acquisitions and disposals based on market cycles, it's evident that aligning your investment activities with these phases can significantly enhance returns and mitigate risks. For example, purchasing a property in the recovery phase—when the market begins to bounce back from a downturn—can result in substantial appreciation as the market progresses into the next growth phase.

Here's what you can do to time your investments strategically:

- Start with thorough research and due diligence on current market conditions.
- Monitor economic indicators closely, such as employment rates, GDP growth, and consumer confidence indices.

- Consult with industry experts and leverage technology tools like market analytics and forecasting software.
- Be prepared to act swiftly when the data suggests an optimal entry or exit point in the cycle.

Evaluating historical data alongside current economic indicators allows investors to gauge their position within the market cycle. Historical patterns often repeat, and observing previous cycles can offer valuable insights. For instance, reviewing how market trends responded to past economic shifts—such as changes in interest rates or regulatory environments—can provide clues about future market direction.

For example, during periods of economic expansion, commercial properties in prime locations tend to perform well. In contrast, during economic recessions, there might be a surge in defaults and foreclosures, creating buying opportunities.

Analyzing this data helps investors refine their strategies and allocate resources more effectively.

Implementing proactive measures during different phases of market cycles optimizes the performance and resilience of real estate investments. During growth phases, focusing on property enhancements, such as upgrades or energy-efficient improvements, can increase rental income and property value. Diversifying your tenant mix and securing long-term leases can also stabilize cash flow.

During downturns, maintaining liquidity and reducing operating costs becomes crucial. This can involve renegotiating service contracts, implementing cost-saving technologies, or even temporarily lowering rents to retain good tenants, thus ensuring steady occupancy rates.

Here's what you can do to implement these proactive measures effectively:

- Regularly review and adjust your property management practices to ensure efficiency.
- Build strong relationships with service providers and contractors to negotiate better terms.
- Explore financing options to maintain liquidity, such as lines of credit or refinancing existing loans.
- Stay adaptable and ready to pivot strategies based on changing market conditions.

By adopting a data-driven approach, investors can navigate the complexities of commercial real estate markets with greater confidence. As market conditions evolve, being attuned to market indicators—like vacancy rates, rental yields, and supply-demand dynamics—enables investors to adapt their strategies accordingly.

It's not just about riding the waves but steering your investment ship with precision, backed by empirical evidence. Whether it's optimizing asset performance during growth phases or safeguarding against downturns, making decisions anchored in evidence increases the likelihood of achieving long-term wealth accumulation.

In conclusion, studying market indicators, adapting strategies to cyclical patterns, and leveraging opportunities presented by market fluctuations are key components for building a resilient and profitable commercial real estate portfolio. Through diligent analysis and strategic planning, investors can better align their actions with the natural rhythms of market cycles, thus maximizing returns while minimizing risks.

Remember, commercial real estate investment is not only about seizing opportunities but also about mitigating potential pitfalls. By prioritizing human welfare and ethical practices, while balancing economic growth, investors contribute positively to their communities and set the stage for sustainable success.

Implementing Tax Strategies for Long-Term Financial Gains

When it comes to long-term wealth accumulation through commercial real estate holdings, implementing savvy tax strategies is paramount. One of the most effective areas where investors can optimize their financial outcomes is by utilizing tax-efficient structures and incentives. Keeping depreciation allowances and 1031 exchanges in mind can significantly reduce tax liabilities and enhance overall returns.

Depreciation is a powerful tool that allows you to deduct the cost of wear and tear on your property over time. The government recognizes that buildings don't last forever, and this acknowledgment can play to your advantage. By applying depreciation allowances, you effectively lower your taxable income which in turn reduces your tax bill. For instance, if you've acquired a commercial property with a value subject to depreciation, you can annually write off a portion of its value, capitalizing on these deductions to buffer against taxable income generated from rent or other income streams related to the property.

To maximize depreciation benefits:

- Make sure to classify each component of the property individually, as different components may depreciate at different rates.
- Engage a qualified accountant who specializes in real estate to ensure accurate and compliant application of depreciation rules.

Another vital strategy is engaging in 1031 exchanges, which allow you to defer capital gains taxes when you sell a property and reinvest the proceeds into a new, like-kind property. This provision ensures that more of your capital remains in play, enabling compounding returns and greater buying power for new investments.

For optimal use of 1031 exchanges:

- Begin by identifying potential replacement properties early within the allowed identification period.
- Work closely with experienced intermediaries who can guide you through the complexities of these transactions.
- Ensure adherence to all IRS regulations and timelines to avoid disqualification of the exchange.

Moving beyond just using depreciation and 1031 exchanges, proper tax planning becomes a cornerstone of maximizing profits, preserving wealth, and enhancing cash flow from your commercial real estate ventures. The foresight in tax planning doesn't just shield you from hefty tax bills; it enhances liquidity and provides financial buffers for unforeseen expenses or investment opportunities.

Strategic tax planning involves laying out a roadmap that aligns with your investment goals. It's about being proactive rather than reactive:
- Review your portfolio regularly to understand how changes in your holdings affect your tax obligations.
- Consider setting aside funds in tax-advantaged accounts to offset future tax liabilities.
- Keep an eye on state and local tax codes, as they can offer additional opportunities for savings.

Understanding the tax implications attached to property investments equips you with the knowledge needed for informed decision-making and long-term wealth preservation. Each decision, be it buying, selling, or holding onto property, carries tax consequences. Savvy investors analyze these implications meticulously to ensure their decisions align with broader financial objectives.

Consider how the tax landscape influences your strategy:

- Be aware of potential changes in tax legislation that might impact your investments.
- Evaluate the timing of your transactions. The right timing can mean the difference between a significant tax hit and a tax-saving opportunity.
- Analyze the interplay between federal, state, and local taxes to minimize overall tax exposure.

Engaging with tax professionals and staying updated on changing regulations are essential practices for optimizing your tax strategies in real estate ventures. The tax code is complex and constantly evolving. Having a team of seasoned advisors can help navigate this complexity and keep you ahead of regulatory changes that might affect your investments.

Here's what you can do to make sure you're always on top of tax optimization:
- Regularly consult with certified public accountants (CPAs) and tax attorneys specializing in real estate.
- Attend industry seminars or workshops focused on real estate tax strategies.
- Subscribe to reputable industry publications or join professional real estate organizations to stay abreast of the latest developments in tax laws and regulations.

By leveraging tax benefits, implementing comprehensive tax planning strategies, staying compliant with tax laws, and continuously seeking professional advice, you not only protect your investments but also gear them towards sustainable, long-term growth. As you navigate the commercial real estate landscape, remember that an evidence-driven approach — one that scrutinizes data, embraces individual freedom, and upholds social responsibility — will always steer you toward enduring success and stability.

Optimizing Property Management for Sustained Income Growth

Efficient property management practices are the cornerstone of long-term income stability and growth in commercial real estate. This involves more than just basic maintenance; it's about being proactive. By addressing issues before they become costly problems, you not only save money but also build trust with your tenants. Keeping properties in top condition isn't just a facet of good stewardship, it's smart business. Here's what you can do to optimize your property management:

- Regularly inspect and maintain major systems like HVAC, plumbing, and electrical to prevent expensive repairs.
- Implement a detailed maintenance schedule to ensure nothing falls through the cracks.

- Utilize preventive measures such as seasonal servicing to extend the lifespan of equipment and infrastructure.

On top of that, tenant retention programs play a critical role in maintaining steady cash flow. High turnover rates can impose significant costs on property owners—not just in terms of lost rent but also the expenses associated with preparing units for new occupants. Fostering positive relationships with tenants can lead to longer leases and more stable income. Retention strategies could include offering lease renewal incentives, creating community-building initiatives, or providing superior customer service experiences. Listening to tenant feedback and promptly addressing concerns shows them that their satisfaction is valued, which in turn encourages them to stay longer.

In today's world, embracing technology solutions and data-driven analytics can marvelously enhance operational efficiencies and overall property performance. Modern property management software enables streamlined operations, from leasing to service requests. These technologies provide real-time insights into the health of your investment, allowing you to make informed decisions quickly.

Data analytics can spotlight trends that might otherwise go unnoticed, giving you a competitive edge. You can leverage data to optimize everything from energy consumption to rental pricing, ensuring that your property remains attractive to current and potential tenants. Here's how you can integrate technology in your management strategy:

- Use property management software that consolidates all operational tasks in one platform.
- Implement energy-efficient technologies to reduce costs and

appeal to environmentally-conscious tenants.

Moreover, strong relationships with tenants underpin a thriving commercial real estate business. Communication, accessibility, and responsiveness are keys to building these relationships. When tenants feel heard and respected, they're more likely to renew leases, recommend your property, and even tolerate occasional inconveniences.

Maintaining high occupancy rates is vital. A half-empty building doesn't just strain your finances; it affects the atmosphere and perception of the property. Tenants are looking for vibrant, well-occupied spaces where their businesses can thrive. To achieve this, cultivate a reliable network of brokers and real estate agents who can help fill vacancies swiftly.

It's crucial to respond promptly to tenant needs, be it repair requests or general inquiries. Speedy and efficient responses demonstrate respect and commitment to their well-being.

Here's how you can maintain strong tenant relationships:

- Regularly communicate with tenants through newsletters or meetings to keep them informed about property updates.
- Set up a reliable system for receiving and addressing maintenance requests.
- Create an online portal where tenants can easily submit requests and track their status.

Continual performance monitoring, strategic planning, and adapting to market dynamics are non-negotiable for optimizing property management outcomes. The real estate market is fluid; what works today may not work tomorrow. Staying ahead of market trends and economic changes allows you to pivot strategies as needed, minimizing risks and maximizing returns.

Performance monitoring involves regularly reviewing financial statements, occupancy rates, and other key performance indicators (KPIs). Are operating costs creeping upward? Is there a decline in tenant inquiries? Such insights can guide timely interventions. By continually assessing your property's performance, you can identify weak spots early and take corrective actions.

Strategic planning involves setting both short-term and long-term goals for your property. Whether it's increasing occupancy by a certain percentage within a year or achieving specific cost-saving targets, having clear objectives fosters a proactive rather than reactive approach.

Adapting to market dynamics means staying informed about industry trends and economic shifts. Factors such as changes in local zoning laws, interest rates, and demographic shifts can significantly impact property values and income potential. Being nimble and ready to evolve with these conditions ensures sustained success.

Here's how to effectively monitor and adapt:

- Regularly review market reports and industry news to stay informed about changes and trends.
- Conduct periodic reviews of your financial performance and adjust your strategies accordingly.
- Network with industry professionals to gain insights and advice on emerging market dynamics.

To wrap it all up, prioritizing property upkeep, utilizing innovative management tools, fostering tenant engagement, and embracing proactive management strategies create a strong foundation for driving sustained income growth in commercial real estate. Remember, the goal isn't just to manage; it's to excel in managing. Taking the time to implement efficient practices, leveraging technology, and building meaningful relationships will pay dividends in the long run, securing your position as a successful real estate investor.

By following these guidelines, you'll not only enhance the value and performance of your properties but will also contribute positively to the communities where your buildings stand, aligning personal profit with social responsibility—a win-win scenario.

Achieving Long-Term Prosperity Through Strategic Real Estate Investments

Creating long-term wealth through commercial real estate hinges on understanding and implementing key strategies. Throughout this chapter, we have explored the importance of diversifying your real estate portfolio to stabilize returns, the significance of recognizing market cycles, leveraging tax strategies for financial gains, and optimizing property management for sustained income growth.

Returning to our initial point, diversification remains a fundamental approach to insulating your investments against market volatility.

By spreading your holdings across different property types and regions, you enhance your ability to weather economic fluctuations while capitalizing on various growth opportunities. This strategy is not only about risk mitigation but also about setting a solid foundation for consistent income streams.

It is clear that the effective timing of acquisitions and disposals based on market cycle phases can greatly influence investment outcomes. Recognizing growth, decline, and recovery stages allows investors to make informed decisions, thereby maximizing returns while reducing potential risks. This awareness equips you with the foresight needed to navigate the complexities of the real estate market more adeptly.

Concerns may arise for some readers regarding the intricacies of tax strategies and the evolving nature of tax laws. While these aspects can be daunting, they are crucial for preserving and enhancing wealth.

Proper tax planning, including the use of depreciation allowances and 1031 exchanges, plays an essential role in reducing liabilities and ensuring your investments remain profitable over the long term.

On a broader scale, efficient property management cannot be overlooked. The upkeep of properties, fostering tenant relations, and embracing technological advancements ensure stable cash flows and enhance property value. This, in turn, contributes positively to local communities, supporting economic growth and development.

As you continue to explore opportunities in commercial real estate, remember that success lies in consistently applying these principles. Whether it's diversifying your holdings, keenly observing market cycles, adopting savvy tax strategies, or managing properties efficiently, the goal is to build a resilient portfolio designed for long-term prosperity. Real estate investment is not just about immediate gains but about crafting a legacy that stands the test of time. Stay informed, remain adaptable, and always keep your end goals within sight.

Chapter 4 - Market Analysis and Forecasting

Market Analysis and Forecasting

Navigating the multifaceted world of real estate investment requires more than just intuition; it demands a keen understanding of the market's underlying forces. Imagine being able to predict the ebbs and flows of commercial property values with a level of accuracy that guides sound, profitable investments. This chapter illuminates how market analysis and forecasting serve as indispensable tools in this pursuit, offering investors a roadmap to informed decision-making.

Economic indicators provide the foundation for this understanding but can often seem like an obscure array of numbers if not analyzed correctly. For instance, consider how GDP growth and employment rates signal the economic health of a region, influencing both property demand and prices. When GDP rises, businesses grow and expand, driving up the need for commercial spaces. Conversely, stagnation or decline warns of potential dips in property values. Employment rates, too, play a critical role; lower unemployment typically means higher consumer spending and robust commercial districts, leading to increased property values. These indicators are intertwined, creating a complex yet navigable tapestry of economic health that directly affects real estate investments.

This chapter delves into identifying and interpreting these vital economic indicators, from GDP and employment statistics to interest rates, consumer spending patterns, and inflation. Each indicator will be unpacked to reveal how it impacts commercial property values and what investors can do to leverage this information. By examining real-world examples and practical steps, the chapter aims to equip you with the knowledge to anticipate market trends and make strategic investment decisions. Whether you're an entrepreneur diversifying your portfolio or an individual looking for value-added opportunities, this exploration promises to enhance your ability to navigate the commercial real estate market successfully.

Understanding Economic Indicators Affecting Commercial Property Values

Understanding economic indicators affecting commercial property values is crucial for anyone looking to make informed decisions in real estate investments. In this context, let's dive right into how various economic variables interplay to shape the market landscape.

Economic indicators such as GDP growth and employment rates are fundamental in gauging the overall health of an economy, and they unavoidably influence property demand and pricing. When Gross Domestic Product (GDP) rises, it signifies enhanced economic productivity and signals stronger business performance. This, in turn, translates into higher demand for commercial properties as businesses seek to expand their operations. On the flip side, stagnation or a decline in GDP might forewarn investors about potential dips in property values. Similarly, robust employment rates often correlate with increased income levels, leading to higher consumer spending and consequently, thriving commercial districts. When people have jobs, they spend more, and businesses flourish, pushing up the demand—and prices—of commercial real estate.

Shifting the focus to another pivotal aspect: interest rates. Monitoring interest rates helps immensely in predicting investment opportunities and understanding property financing costs. Interest rates fundamentally impact borrowing costs. Lower rates often make financing cheaper, encouraging both developers and buyers to invest in commercial properties. Conversely, when interest rates rise, the cost of borrowing also escalates, potentially dampening investment enthusiasm.

Here is what you can do in order to achieve the goal:

- If interest rates are expected to decrease, anticipate more favorable financing terms and consider investing soon to take advantage of cheaper loans.
- Keep tabs on central bank announcements and economic reports that hint at future rate changes.
- Evaluate the long-term implications of fixed versus variable-rate loans in relation to your investment strategy.
- Balance your investment portfolio by considering both short-term gains from lower interest rates and long-term stability.

Let's move on to a rather insightful indicator – consumer spending patterns. Analyzing these patterns can significantly guide decisions regarding property types and locations. Consumer spending is a reflection of economic confidence. When consumers are willing to spend more, retail and entertainment sectors benefit, making commercial properties in high-footfall areas particularly valuable. Observing trends, such as an increase in online shopping, could indicate a higher demand for logistics centers over traditional retail spaces. Similarly, a surge in spending on dining out may signal great opportunities in developing restaurant-focused commercial properties.

To leverage consumer spending data:
- Examine local and national retail sales reports to identify booming sectors.
- Study demographic changes; younger populations might show different spending habits compared to older generations.
- Pay attention to shifts towards experiential spending; properties

that offer unique experiences might be in higher demand.

- Use consumer surveys and feedback to gauge preferences, tailoring your investments accordingly.

Equally important is studying inflation rates. Inflation affects not only the immediate cost of goods and services but also holds significant implications for the long-term value preservation of real estate assets. During periods of high inflation, commodity prices soar, which can lead to increased construction costs and subsequently higher property prices. However, for existing property owners, inflation can contribute to asset appreciation over time. Rental incomes often adjust with inflation, thus offering a hedge against its eroding effects. Yet, exceedingly high inflation could deter new investments due to unpredictability in returns.

To assess and navigate through inflation:
- Track inflation indices like the Consumer Price Index (CPI) for up-to-date information.
- Consider implementing lease agreements that include inflation-linked rent adjustments.
- Diversify your portfolio to offset risk; properties in different sectors may respond differently to inflation.
- Remain cautious of hyperinflation environments where even property values might struggle to keep pace.

In summary, understanding and vigilantly monitoring these economic indicators provide invaluable insights into market trends. They enable investors to make strategic and well-informed decisions. By keeping a finger on the pulse of GDP growth, employment rates, interest rates, consumer spending, and inflation, one can preemptively strategize and position investments to not just survive but thrive amidst varying economic conditions.

Remember, the objective here isn't merely about accruing wealth through property acquisition but doing so in a manner that promotes sustainable growth and human welfare. Whether you're an entrepreneur diversifying your portfolio or an individual seeking value-added opportunities in commercial real estate, empirical evidence should be at the core of your decision-making process. When done right, leveraging these economic indicators ensures a balanced approach where economic growth complements human welfare, forging a path to lasting financial success and societal well-being.

Implementing Predictive Analytics for Anticipating Market Trends

Utilizing market analysis for informed decision-making in real estate investments isn't just a matter of gut feeling or luck—it's about leveraging the power of predictive analytics to make data-driven decisions. Let's dive into how you can harness historical data and statistical models to forecast future property values.

Predictive analytics starts with understanding the past. By utilizing historical data, we can spot trends and patterns that might not be immediately obvious. For instance, consider the fluctuations in property prices over the past decade in a given market. This data can reveal cycles and significant events that influenced these changes. Here's what you can do to incorporate such insights:

- **Gather comprehensive historical data** : Look at various sources, including government databases, local council records, and private property market analyses.
- **Analyze trends over time** : Identify periods of growth and decline, and match them with external factors such as economic

policies, interest rates, and demographic shifts.

- **Apply statistical models** : Use regression analysis and time-series forecasting to make sense of the data and project future property values.

When you have a robust dataset, applying machine learning algorithms becomes the next step. Machine learning can uncover hidden patterns and predict future trends more accurately than traditional methods. You see, unlike basic statistical models, machine learning algorithms are adaptive; they learn from new data continuously. To effectively use machine learning in real estate investment:

- **Select the right algorithm** : Depending on your objectives, choose between supervised learning models like Linear Regression or unsupervised ones like Clustering.

- **Train your model with historical data** : Divide your dataset into training and testing sets to ensure the model learns accurately without overfitting.
- **Validate and refine your model** : Continuously update your model with new data to improve its predictive accuracy.

With a solid understanding of historical trends and advanced pattern recognition through machine learning, you can now adjust your investment strategies based on evolving market conditions. Predictive analytics allows you to react dynamically as opposed to sticking to rigid long-term plans that might become outdated. Here's how to adapt your investment strategies:

- **Monitor key indicators** : Keep an eye on leading indicators pertinent to the real estate market, such as unemployment rates, GDP growth, and housing start rates.
- **Run scenario analyses** : Use your predictive models to simulate

different market conditions (e.g., economic downturns, policy changes) and see how various properties fare.
- **Adjust your portfolio accordingly** : Based on the outcomes of your simulations, shift your investments towards properties expected to perform better under anticipated market conditions.

Risk analysis is another critical element to enhance the accuracy of your predictions. Incorporating risk into your predictive models ensures that you're not only looking at potential gains but also preparing for possible setbacks. Effective risk analysis involves multiple layers:

- **Identify potential risks** : These could range from economic downturns to regulatory changes, and even natural disasters.
- **Quantify risks** : Assign probabilities to different risk

scenarios using your historical and current data.

- **Incorporate risk metrics into your models** : Metrics like Value-at-Risk (VaR) or Conditional Value-at-Risk (CVaR) can help you understand the likelihood and impact of adverse events on your investments.

By integrating risk analysis into your predictive models, you get a more realistic picture of both opportunities and threats. This balanced approach allows for better preparedness and resilience against market volatility.

To sum it up, predictive analytics provides a powerful toolkit for making informed real estate investment decisions. The ability to anticipate market trends through historical data, machine learning, and risk analysis means you can adapt swiftly and optimize your investment outcomes. Embracing these evidence-driven techniques doesn't only help in growing wealth but also aligns with a sense of social responsibility by promoting stable and informed market behaviors. Remember, the more accurate your predictions, the better positioned you'll be to navigate the complexities of the real estate market.

By embedding these practices into your investment strategy, you ensure that each move you make is calculated, informed, and strategically sound. And who knows? Maybe this will also be part of the broader effort needed to foster a less polarized, more cooperative society where personal freedom and collective responsibility coexist harmoniously.

Assessing Demand-Supply Dynamics in Key Markets

To assess the demand-supply dynamics in key markets, it's crucial first to understand population growth trends. Population growth is a powerful determinant of future demand for commercial properties. When people migrate to a particular area, they not only require accommodations but also stimulate local businesses and services. This creates additional demand for office spaces, retail outlets, and hospitality services.

Take urban centers like Austin, Texas, or Seattle, Washington, which have seen significant influxes of residents over the past decade. Analyzing such trends can give you valuable insights into where the market is heading. Here's what you can do in order to gauge future demand:

- Look at census data to identify areas with rising populations.
- Consider migration patterns, especially those driven by job opportunities, quality of life, and affordability.
- Assess local government policies that might be attracting new residents, such as tax incentives or improved infrastructure.
- Evaluate the economic activities driving these demographic changes, whether it's tech hubs,

manufacturing corridors, or educational institutions.

By understanding where people are moving, you can predict which areas will see increased demand for commercial properties. This approach allows you to get ahead of the curve rather than chasing trends.

Next, evaluating new construction projects is vital for anticipating supply fluctuations in specific market segments. New developments are often signs of optimism in the market. However, an excess of new constructions can lead to oversupply, which may impact rental rates and property values negatively.

For instance, if you're considering investing in warehouse properties, look into any upcoming industrial park developments within the area. Similarly, when eyeing retail spaces, monitor the planned construction of shopping malls or mixed-use buildings.

Here's how you can keep tabs on new construction projects:
- Review planning commission records and building permits to see what projects are in the pipeline.
- Attend local government meetings where new construction approvals are discussed.
- Network with real estate developers and contractors to get insider information on upcoming projects.
- Utilize online platforms that track construction activities and market reports from real estate firms.

By keeping abreast of what's being built, you can better anticipate future supply levels and adjust your investment strategies accordingly. Understanding these dynamics helps mitigate risks and leverage opportunities as they arise.

The next aspect involves analyzing vacancy rates and absorption rates to assess market equilibrium and potential investment opportunities.

Vacancy rates reflect how many properties are available versus how many are occupied. Conversely, absorption rates indicate the pace at which available properties are being rented out or sold.

High vacancy rates can signal an oversupply or lack of demand, whereas low vacancy rates typically suggest a healthy demand. Absorption rates provide a clearer picture of market activity—how quickly space is taken up once it becomes available. These metrics are essential for determining the balance between supply and demand in the market.

Here's how you can analyze these rates effectively:

- Gather data from reliable sources such as real estate market reports, industry surveys, and property management firms.
- Compare historical data to identify trends over time. Are vacancy rates increasing or decreasing? How fast are properties being absorbed?

- Pay attention to seasonal variations that might affect these metrics. For instance, retail spaces might show different trends during holiday seasons compared to other times of the year.
- Consider the geographic scope of your analysis. Rates can vary significantly between neighborhoods, cities, and even within different parts of a single city.

By regularly monitoring these indicators, you can spot opportunities to invest in under-supplied markets or avoid areas with high vacancy rates and slow absorption. This ensures your investments align with current market conditions, maximizing returns.

Lastly, studying demographic shifts and urban development plans helps identify emerging market hotspots. Demographic data includes factors such as age distribution, income levels, education attainment, and household sizes. Urban development plans encompass infrastructure projects, zoning changes, and community initiatives that can transform neighborhoods.

Areas experiencing demographic shifts, such as an influx of younger professionals or retirees, often see corresponding increases in demand for certain types of commercial properties. Young professionals might drive demand for co-working spaces and trendy retail locations, while an aging population could heighten the need for healthcare facilities and senior living centers.

To tap into these emerging hotspots, consider the following steps:

- Analyze demographic data available through public records, academic research, and market studies.
- Monitor announcements of major urban development projects like new transit systems, cultural hubs, or business districts.

- Engage with local communities and stakeholders to understand their visions and concerns about ongoing developments.
- Evaluate the long-term potential of these changes and how they align with broader economic trends.

By leveraging this information, you can position yourself to invest in areas poised for significant growth, ensuring that you capitalize on early opportunities before the market becomes saturated.

In essence, assessing demand-supply dynamics through these lenses —population growth trends, new construction projects, vacancy and absorption rates, and demographic shifts—provides a comprehensive understanding of the market. By doing so, you target lucrative investment opportunities and maximize returns.

Balancing evidence-driven insights with individual and social responsibilities remains key. Ensuring that economic growth does not overshadow human welfare aligns both aspects harmoniously. As you navigate the commercial real estate landscape, let empirical evidence guide your decisions, considering personal and community well-being at every turn. This way, we can foster sustainable growth, enriching both our portfolios and the society at large.

Incorporating Competitive Analysis for Strategic Positioning

When it comes to real estate investments, the practice of market analysis is crucial. One effective method is conducting competitor analysis to identify market gaps and differentiation strategies. In essence, this means understanding what your competitors are doing well and where they are falling short. For example, if every property in your target area offers high-end amenities but lacks eco-friendly features, that's a gap you could exploit.

Here is what you can do to achieve this goal:

- Start by gathering data on competing properties in your chosen market. This includes looking into their pricing strategies, tenant profiles, and unique selling propositions.
- Make use of online real estate platforms and databases to collect this information. Visiting competitor websites and attending open houses can also provide valuable insights.
- Analyze customer reviews and feedback on these properties. This can highlight areas where competitors are underperforming.
- Use this information to carve out your niche. Ask yourself how you can offer something distinct that fulfills an unmet need or improves on what's already available.

Similarly, benchmarking rental rates and property performance metrics against industry peers can give you a solid footing. This involves comparing your property's financial performance and operational metrics with those of similar properties. Understanding the average rental rate in your area ensures that you're not pricing yourself out of the market or leaving money on the table.

Here's what you can do in order to benchmark effectively:

- First, gather rental rate data from multiple sources like local real estate listings, property management firms, and market surveys.
- Then, compare occupancy rates and lease renewal percentages. These figures will tell you whether your pricing strategy is attracting and retaining tenants effectively.
- Another metric worth exploring is the cost per square foot for maintenance and utilities. By keeping these costs competitive, you can offer better value without sacrificing profit margins.

While monitoring market trends and industry developments doesn't require a step-by-step guideline, its importance can't be understated. Staying ahead of competitors means keeping a pulse on the latest shifts in the real estate landscape. Regularly reading industry reports, subscribing to real estate newsletters, and attending trade shows or webinars can keep you informed about emerging trends. It allows you to pivot your strategy according to changes in consumer behavior, regulatory updates, or technological advancements.

Being up-to-date with these trends provides a significant advantage. For example, if there's a rising demand for co-working spaces within commercial properties due to the gig economy's boom, knowing this beforehand enables you to adapt swiftly. You can reposition your property to meet this growing need, thereby attracting a new segment of tenants who might otherwise turn to your competitors.

Beyond just trend-spotting, leveraging competitive insights can substantially fine-tune your marketing and leasing strategies for optimal property positioning. The idea is to take the knowledge you've gained from your competitor analysis and market monitoring and apply it to enhance your property's appeal.

For instance, if your competitors offer basic amenities at a certain price point, you might choose to provide additional services such as fitness centers, community events, or advanced security features—all while maintaining a competitive price. Crafting your marketing messages around these enhanced features can make your property stand out.

To implement these strategies effectively:

- Tailor your advertising to emphasize what makes your property unique. Highlight the added benefits tenants will enjoy compared to other options in the market.

- Utilize various media channels where potential tenants are most active. Social media, real estate forums, and local publications can all be effective.
- Invest in quality visuals and virtual tours. In today's digital age, an impressive online presence can often sway tenant decisions more than traditional methods.
- Constantly collect feedback from current tenants. Their experiences can provide fresh insights on areas for improvement, ensuring you stay a step ahead of competitors.

The key takeaway here is clear: Competitive analysis isn't just a supplementary tool—it's a critical component of successful real estate investment. By identifying market gaps, benchmarking performance, staying on top of industry trends, and leveraging these insights to refine your strategies, you establish a robust foundation for profitability.

Furthermore, incorporating these practices helps ensure that economic growth in your investments aligns seamlessly with human welfare considerations. Providing more tailored, desirable housing options benefits both the investor and the community at large. When executed correctly, it's possible to balance individual freedom with social responsibility, creating a win-win scenario for everyone involved.

In conclusion, the integration of comprehensive competitive analysis into your real estate strategy is indispensable. It equips you with the tools to navigate a crowded market, offering unmatched opportunities to differentiate your offerings and maximize returns. Remember, an evidence-driven approach grounded in thorough research and strategic planning can decidedly tilt the scales in your favor. Investing time and resources into these analyses will ultimately shape your trajectory toward sustained success in the real estate sector.

Strategic Approaches to Market Analysis and Forecasting

In this chapter, we have delved into the multifaceted world of market analysis and how its strategic application can significantly enhance decision-making in real estate investments. We've explored various economic indicators like GDP growth, employment rates, interest rates, consumer spending patterns, and inflation, each offering unique insights into market trends and opportunities.

From our discussion, it's clear that understanding these economic indicators is not just beneficial but essential for making informed investment decisions. In the introduction, we emphasized the importance of empirical evidence as the foundation for strategic planning, a theme that has been consistently echoed throughout the chapter. As we conclude, it's vital to reiterate that data-driven insights can shape successful real estate ventures, fostering both financial growth and societal benefits.

However, readers might wonder about the challenges posed by the dynamic nature of economic variables. Economic conditions can change rapidly, influenced by global events, policy shifts, and unforeseen circumstances. This unpredictability underscores the need for continuous monitoring and adaptive strategies. Investors must stay vigilant, continuously updating their models and analysis to reflect the latest data and trends.

On a broader scale, relying on robust market analysis can contribute to more stable and resilient real estate markets. By making well-informed decisions, investors help stabilize property values and occupancy rates, benefiting not just individual portfolios but also the communities where they invest. In doing so, they promote economic stability and support local economies, ultimately leading to sustainable development and improved quality of life.

As you move forward, consider the interplay between meticulous market analysis and the broader impacts of your investment choices. While the goal remains to expand wealth, there's an equally important objective of ensuring that such growth aligns with community welfare and sustainable practices. By investing thoughtfully, guided by solid data and predictive analytics, you set the stage for long-term success and positive societal contributions.

Ultimately, the journey of real estate investment is one of constant learning and adaptation. Embrace the insights gleaned from economic indicators, stay attuned to market dynamics, and remain agile in your strategies. This balanced approach will not only enhance your investment outcomes but also contribute to a more equitable and prosperous society.

Chapter 5 - Financial Analysis Techniques

Financial Analysis Techniques

Navigating the commercial real estate market can often seem like deciphering a complex puzzle, requiring not just strategic insight but also a firm grasp of financial analysis. Investors who excel in this landscape understand that scrutinizing every aspect of an investment is pivotal to their success. This chapter dives deep into the array of financial analysis techniques essential for making informed decisions and maximizing returns on commercial real estate investments.

One cornerstone of effective financial analysis is assessing cash flows—carefully tracking all income and expenses related to a property. Imagine acquiring a commercial property without fully understanding its cash flow dynamics. An investor might overlook seasonal fluctuations in rental income or underestimate ongoing maintenance costs, leading to financial strain. For example, securing a property with high initial returns might seem appealing, but without a thorough analysis, an investor could miss underlying issues such as significant future repair costs or inconsistent tenant payments. Consequently, mastering cash flow analysis becomes indispensable, allowing investors to foresee potential challenges and plan accordingly.

In this chapter, we will explore various financial analysis tools and techniques essential for commercial real estate investments. We begin by delving into cash flow analysis, breaking down how to meticulously track income and expenses to get a clear picture of profitability. Following that, we will discuss calculating Return on Investment (ROI) for property acquisitions—a vital metric for comparing different opportunities and ensuring lucrative investments. Additionally, we will cover risk assessment models, helping you identify and mitigate potential risks.

Finally, we'll navigate budgeting and forecasting methods to ensure robust financial planning. Each section aims to equip investors with the knowledge required to make well-informed, strategic decisions in the ever-changing commercial real estate market.

Understanding the Importance of Cash Flow Analysis

Understanding the importance of cash flow analysis in evaluating investment properties is pivotal for anyone considering commercial real estate investments. At its core, cash flow analysis provides a clear snapshot of potential profitability by meticulously examining all incoming and outgoing funds.

When investors delve into cash flow analysis, they gain a nuanced understanding of how money moves in and out of an investment property. This granular view enables them to identify whether a property is generating enough income to cover its expenses and, ideally, yield profit. Cash flow isn't just about seeing money come in; it's about understanding the timing of these inflows and outflows, which is crucial for managing any financial undertakings effectively.

Assessing cash flow doesn't stop at profitability evaluation. It extends to making well-informed decisions regarding property acquisitions. Here's what you can do to leverage cash flow for informed decision-making:

- Gather comprehensive data on all revenue streams associated with the property, such as rent, lease payments, and other income sources.
- Track all expenses meticulously, including mortgage payments, maintenance costs, utilities, property taxes, and insurance premiums.
- Calculate the net cash flow by subtracting total expenses from total income.

- Analyze historical cash flow data if available, to spot trends and patterns that might impact future performance.
- Use this information to gauge the financial health of the property and decide if it meets your investment criteria.

By assessing cash flow, investors also evaluate the overall financial health of a property. Think of it as a financial report card. If a property demonstrates consistent positive cash flow, it often indicates sound financial management and robustness. Conversely, if a property struggles with negative cash flow, it suggests potential issues that may need addressing. Effective use of cash flow assessments can thus help investors avoid problematic properties and reinforce their portfolio with financially viable assets.

Understanding cash flow patterns can be immensely beneficial in predicting future income streams too.

For instance, seasonal variations in rental income might signal periods when additional financial reserves are needed. Recognizing these patterns helps in identifying areas where financial management can be honed. Here's how you can navigate this:

- Regularly update and review cash flow statements to maintain accuracy.
- Look for cyclical trends or anomalies and correlate them with events or market conditions.
- Plan for fluctuations by setting aside reserves during peak cash flow periods to offset leaner times.
- Adjust strategies based on insights gained from pattern recognition to enhance financial stability.

Cash flow analysis remains indispensable when it comes to budgeting and forecasting for real estate ventures. A carefully executed cash flow analysis aids investors in creating realistic budgets that account for all expected revenues and expenses. This foresight prevents shortfalls that could jeopardize the sustainability of a venture. To ensure your real estate investments remain viable:

- Incorporate projected cash flow analyses into your annual planning cycles.
- Align your budgeting process with cash flow forecasts to match incomes with upcoming expenditures.
- Utilize scenario analyses to test how different situations might affect your cash flows.
- Adapt your strategy as needed to maintain positive cash flow and meet financial goals.

In light of these steps, one can see that cash flow analysis serves as a critical tool in the arsenal of commercial real estate investors. It enhances the ability to make astute decisions, health-checks properties, predicts future financial scenarios, and ensures sustained viability through effective budgeting.

The key takeaway here is simple and clear: Investors should regularly conduct cash flow analyses. This practice not only optimizes financial performance but also guides strategic decision-making. Regular reviews of cash flow statements keep one attuned to the financial pulse of their investments. This proactive approach underpins successful and sustainable real estate ventures, empowering investors to navigate the intricacies of the market with confidence.

Understanding and utilizing cash flow analysis unlocks a realm of opportunities, while safeguarding against potential pitfalls. It is, without a shadow of a doubt, a foundational aspect of achieving financial mastery in commercial real estate investments.

Learning How to Calculate ROI for Property Acquisitions

Calculating ROI for property acquisitions is pivotal for any savvy investor aiming to navigate the commercial real estate landscape with precision. It serves as a beacon, guiding decisions and illuminating the path toward profitable ventures. Let's delve into why this practice is indispensable and how it can be meticulously applied to maximize returns.

ROI calculations help investors assess the profitability of a property relative to the initial investment. At its core, ROI—or Return on Investment—is an equation that provides a percentage reflecting the profit earned from an investment relative to its cost. Here's why that's essential: by quantifying profitability, investors gain a clear picture of whether a property is a lucrative opportunity or a drain on resources. To calculate ROI, you can use the following formula:

- Subtract the initial investment cost from the final value of the investment.
- Divide this figure by the initial investment cost.

- Multiply the result by 100 to get a percentage.

For instance, if you bought a property for $500,000 and sold it later for $700,000, your ROI would be calculated as follows:

- ($700,000 - $500,000) / $500,000 = 0.4
- 0.4 x 100 = 40%

This 40% indicates that you've made a 40% return on your initial investment, a clear indicator of the property's profitability.

By determining ROI, investors can compare different investment opportunities and prioritize those with higher returns. In the bustling world of commercial real estate, opportunities abound, but not all are created equal. Some may promise high returns but come with considerable risks; others might offer steady, moderate returns with minimal hassle. Understanding and calculating ROI empowers investors to weigh these options against each other. Suppose you have two potential properties—one promises a 30% ROI and the other a 15% ROI. The higher percentage speaks volumes, guiding you toward the more profitable venture. However, it's crucial to consider other factors like risk, market conditions, and personal investment goals before making a final decision.

Understanding ROI enables investors to evaluate the effectiveness of their capital allocation strategies and make adjustments accordingly. This isn't just about picking the best new investment; it's also a tool for refining ongoing strategies. If you notice that properties in certain markets consistently deliver better ROIs, it might be wise to shift more resources into those areas. Conversely, low or negative ROIs signal properties or strategies that need rethinking. To ensure you're making the most informed decisions, regularly revisit these calculations and adjust your strategies based on current data.

Monitoring ROI over time allows investors to track performance trends and make informed decisions for portfolio growth. An isolated ROI calculation provides a snapshot, but tracking ROI over periods furnishes a narrative. Are your investments growing more profitable or tapering off? Are market shifts affecting your returns? By continually monitoring ROI, you arm yourself with insights to forecast future trends and pivot when necessary. It's akin to maintaining a health check on your investment portfolio, ensuring each component contributes positively to your financial objectives.

As we weave through these concepts, the underlying theme becomes clear: Calculating ROI is essential for assessing the financial viability of real estate investments and maximizing returns. Embracing a systematic approach to ROI calculations allows you to demystify the financial aspects of property investments, leading to smarter, evidence-driven decisions.

To illustrate further, let's explore an example of ROI application in commercial real estate. Imagine you're considering investing in a small retail center. You initially purchase the property for $1 million. Over the next three years, you invest an additional $200,000 for renovations and improvements. After these enhancements, the net operating income (NOI)—which represents the property's earnings after operating expenses—rises to $150,000 annually. Now your total investment is $1.2 million.

Here's what you can do in order to achieve the goal:

- **Calculate the Total Return**: Determine the net profit by multiplying the annual NOI by the holding period, say three years. In this case, it's $150,000 x 3 = $450,000.

- **Determine the Initial Investment**: Sum the purchase price and renovation costs—$1 million + $200,000 = $1.2 million.
- **Compute the ROI**: Use the ROI formula to find the profitability percentage. ($450,000 - $1.2 million) / $1.2 million = 0.375, or 37.5%.

This exercise reveals a substantial 37.5% ROI, indicating a robust return on your commercial real estate venture.

Now, let's broaden our discussion slightly. While ROI is a potent tool, it's part of a larger toolkit needed for sound financial analysis. Other metrics like Net Present Value (NPV), Internal Rate of Return (IRR), and Cash-on-Cash Return provide additional layers of insight. Together, these metrics form a comprehensive picture, helping you navigate the complexities of commercial real estate with confidence.

NPV calculates the present value of future cash flows compared to the initial investment, factoring in a chosen discount rate. IRR, on the other hand, identifies the rate at which the NPV of all cash flows from an investment equals zero, providing another measure of investment profitability. Meanwhile, Cash-on-Cash Return focuses on the cash income generated compared to the cash invested, giving a more immediate sense of liquidity.

Incorporating these tools alongside ROI nurtures a well-rounded understanding of each investment's merits and pitfalls. You begin to see not just from a single angle but from a multidimensional perspective. It's a blend of art and science, where empirical data meets strategic foresight.

Ultimately, your journey in commercial real estate investments will benefit immensely from disciplined financial analysis. With ROI as your guide, complemented by additional metrics, you'll be better equipped to scrutinize potential investments, allocate your capital wisely, and nurture a thriving portfolio that balances economic growth with human welfare. Remember, the ultimate aim is to foster a strategy that not only yields financial rewards but also aligns with your broader vision and values.

Exploring Risk Assessment Models for Project Evaluations

When diving into commercial real estate investments, one of the most critical aspects investors need to tackle is risk assessment models. These models are not just technical tools; they're pivotal for spotting potential risks and uncertainties inherent in each project. By understanding these, investors can safeguard their capital and potentially increase their returns.

Let's start with understanding how risk assessment models serve as a radar for identifying potential pitfalls. Just like sailing through unpredictable waters requires a reliable map, venturing into the complex world of commercial real estate demands an astute awareness of what risks lie ahead. Whether it's market volatility, changes in interest rates, or tenant risks, these models help paint a comprehensive picture. Enabling investors to think several moves ahead, thus avoiding unexpected financial storms.

Once you've identified potential risks, the next step involves developing contingency plans and strategies to mitigate these risks. Here's a practical approach to tackling this:

- **Start by categorizing risks** : Group them into market risks, financial risks, operational risks, and regulatory risks. This helps break down the complexities, allowing for targeted strategies.

- **Develop specific mitigation strategies** : For example, if you identify market volatility as a significant risk, consider diversifying your investment portfolio. Look at properties across different sectors or geographic locations to spread your exposure.

- **Establish financial buffers** : Ensure that you have sufficient reserves or access to additional funding to cushion against unforeseen financial setbacks.
- **Regularly review and update your strategies** : Markets change, new data emerges, and so should your mitigation strategies. Stay agile and ready to adjust your plans based on the latest insights.

Carrying out these steps ensures that when risks do materialize, you're not caught off guard but instead have preemptive measures in place to address them.

Moreover, a deep understanding of these risk factors enables more informed decision-making and resource allocation. Imagine you've identified that a particular location has a high potential for increased property taxes due to upcoming local government policies. With this insight, you can allocate resources towards lobbying efforts or seek insurance to cover potential increases, ensuring that your project remains financially viable. It's about creating a balance—allocating enough resources to areas that need it while keeping an eye on overall project health.

Next, let's delve into the importance of regularly updating risk assessments. The commercial real estate market is dynamic and ever-changing. New developments, policy changes, or even global economic trends can significantly impact previously stable projects. To keep up, diligent monitoring and updating of your risk assessments are crucial.

Here's a practical guide for ensuring your risk assessments remain current:

- **Set regular review intervals** : Make it a habit to review your risk profiles quarterly or bi-annually.
- **Incorporate new data** : Use recent market reports, industry

analyses, and economic forecasts to inform your updated assessments.

- **Involve stakeholders** : Engage with your team, including property managers, financial analysts, and legal advisors, to get a well-rounded view of potential new risks and updates.
- **Implement technology solutions** : Utilize software tools designed for real-time risk monitoring and analytics. These can provide immediate alerts on any changes needing attention.

By adhering to these guidelines, you stay proactive rather than reactive, which is essential for navigating the volatile landscapes of commercial real estate.

At the end of the day, implementing robust risk assessment models isn't just about protecting your investments; it's about ensuring long-term financial stability. Safeguarding your assets through meticulous planning allows you to focus on growth opportunities with greater confidence. It's akin to having a safety net while performing high-wire acrobatics—the assurance that you won't fall far lets you concentrate fully on reaching new heights.

It's also worth noting the broader implications of thorough risk assessments. When you consider every angle, anticipate potential issues, and prepare for them, you contribute to a more stable and resilient real estate market. This promotes sustainable development and growth within the sector, benefiting not just individual investors but the community at large.

For those looking to expand their wealth through smart investments in commercial real estate or entrepreneurs seeking to diversify their portfolios, these principles offer a solid foundation. Understanding and applying risk assessment models can be the distinguishing factor between a successful venture and a costly misstep.

In conclusion, while economic growth is undeniably important, prioritizing human welfare in the context of judicious risk management leads to sounder investments. This approach aligns personal responsibility with the need for a safety net to safeguard those who encounter difficulties along their journey. After all, investing isn't just about numbers; it's about building a future with both financial and social capital firmly secured.

Mastering Budgeting and Forecasting Methods for Real Estate Ventures

Budgeting and forecasting are crucial components of financial analysis in commercial real estate investments. These tools enable investors to navigate the complexities of the market while maximizing their returns. Let's delve into how mastering these methods can significantly enhance financial management and strategic decision-making.

Budgeting enables investors to allocate resources efficiently and track expenses throughout the investment lifecycle. This is not just about tallying numbers; it's a strategic approach that dictates how and where resources should be deployed to optimize outcomes. Here is what you can do to achieve effective budgeting:

- Begin by identifying all potential income sources and expenditures associated with your real estate venture. This includes purchase costs, renovation expenses, operating costs, and projected rental incomes.
- Next, categorize these expenses into fixed and variable costs. Fixed costs remain constant over time, such as loan payments and property taxes, while variable costs fluctuate, like maintenance and utility charges.
- Create a detailed budget plan covering different phases of the investment: acquisition, operation, and disposition. Make sure to set aside a contingency fund for unexpected expenses.

- Use software tools or spreadsheet programs to maintain and update your budget regularly. This helps in tracking actual expenses against your planned budget, identifying variances, and making necessary adjustments promptly.
- Finally, review and adjust your budget periodically. The real estate market is dynamic, and regular reviews ensure that your budget reflects current market conditions and supports sound financial decisions.

Forecasting future financial performance helps investors anticipate challenges and opportunities, enhancing strategic decision-making. Accurately predicting future trends can spell the difference between success and failure in real estate ventures. Here's how you can make accurate forecasts:

- Start by gathering historical data on property values, occupancy rates, and rental incomes in your target area. This data provides a baseline for projecting future performance.

- Conduct a thorough market analysis to understand current trends and potential factors that could affect property values and demand. Pay attention to economic indicators, local developments, and regulatory changes.

- Develop multiple forecast scenarios – best case, worst case, and most likely case. Each scenario should incorporate different assumptions about key variables like market growth rates, inflation, and interest rates.

- Utilize financial modeling techniques, such as discounted cash flow (DCF) analysis, to estimate future cash flows and property valuations. These models help in understanding the long-term financial implications of your investment decisions.

- Regularly update your forecasts based on new information and market changes. The more frequently you revisit and refine your projections, the more accurate and useful they will be in guiding your strategic choices.

By incorporating budgeting and forecasting, investors can enhance the overall financial management of their real estate ventures. A holistic approach involves integrating these tools into every aspect of your investment strategy. Here's how to do it seamlessly:

- Align your budgeting process with your investment objectives. Whether you aim to maximize short-term gains or generate steady long-term income, your budget should reflect these goals.
- Use forecasts to inform your budget allocations. For instance, if your forecasts indicate rising property prices in a particular area,

you might allocate more resources for acquisitions in that region.

- Implement performance metrics to monitor the effectiveness of your budgeting and forecasting efforts. Key metrics could include return on investment (ROI), net operating income (NOI), and internal rate of return (IRR).
- Foster a culture of financial discipline within your investment team. Encourage regular reviews of budgets and forecasts, and promote transparency and accountability in financial reporting.

Regularly revisiting and adjusting budgets and forecasts based on market dynamics is essential for adapting to changing conditions. The real estate market is known for its cyclical nature, so staying flexible is vital. Here are some steps to keep your financial plans agile:

- Schedule regular reviews of your budget and forecast reports, at least quarterly. This allows you to identify deviations from expectations early and take corrective actions.

- Stay informed about market trends and emerging risks. Subscribe to industry publications, attend seminars, and network with other professionals to keep abreast of changes that could impact your investments.

- Adjust your financial plans proactively rather than reactively. If you foresee potential downturns, consider cost-cutting measures or refinancing options ahead of time.

- Keep communication open with stakeholders, including lenders, tenants, and property managers. Their insights can provide valuable information that enhances your ability to adapt your strategies effectively.

- Document any changes made to your budgets and forecasts, along with the rationale behind them. This builds a historical record that can improve the accuracy of future planning efforts.

Effective budgeting and forecasting are essential tools for achieving financial success and sustainability in commercial real estate investments. They provide a structured framework for managing resources and making informed decisions, ultimately leading to better outcomes.

As we wrap up, it's important to recognize that mastering these tools requires a balance of diligence and adaptability. While data and empirical evidence lay the foundation, the ability to anticipate change and respond swiftly elevates your investment strategy.

Remember, every real estate venture is unique, and so is the path to its success. Equip yourself with robust budgeting and forecasting practices, stay informed, and remain flexible. With these strategies in place, you're well on your way to navigating the commercial real estate landscape with confidence and expertise.

Ultimately, the true power of financial analysis lies not only in the numbers but in the stories they tell and the foresight they enable. As you continue your journey into commercial real estate investments, let these tools guide you toward informed, strategic, and impactful decisions.

Integrating Financial Analysis for Commercial Real Estate Success

In this chapter, we have explored the essential tools and techniques for financial analysis in commercial real estate investments. We've delved into understanding cash flow analysis, calculating Return on Investment (ROI), risk assessment models, and mastering budgeting and forecasting methods. Each of these components plays a pivotal role in making informed decisions and ensuring the success and sustainability of your real estate ventures.

Returning to our initial discussion on cash flow analysis, we see how crucial it is for evaluating the profitability and overall financial health of an investment property. By regularly conducting cash flow analyses, investors can maintain a clear view of their property's financial performance, enabling more strategic decision-making. This practice serves as the foundation for understanding whether an investment is sustainable and profitable over time.

Our position remains clear: mastering these financial tools is indispensable for anyone serious about commercial real estate investing. However, some readers might be concerned about the complexity and effort required to employ these techniques effectively. It's important to acknowledge that while these methods may seem daunting, they are instrumental in safeguarding your investments and maximizing returns.

On a broader scale, failing to integrate comprehensive financial analysis can lead to misguided decisions, underperformance, and potential financial losses. Conversely, disciplined application of these techniques contributes to a more stable, transparent, and efficient real estate market. This not only benefits individual investors but also supports the overall health of the real estate sector, promoting sustainable growth and development.

As you continue your journey into commercial real estate investments, consider these tools your allies. They provide clarity, foresight, and strategic direction. Embrace the process, remain adaptable to changing market conditions, and let data-driven insights guide your decisions. The realm of commercial real estate offers vast opportunities, and with the right financial analysis techniques, you're well-equipped to navigate its complexities successfully. Looking ahead, remember that the key to thriving in real estate lies in blending careful analysis with strategic vision.

Chapter 6 - Exit Strategies for Real Estate Investments

Exit Strategies for Real Estate Investments

Real estate investments are often celebrated for their potential to generate significant returns, but the key to unlocking maximum profitability lies in an often overlooked aspect: exit strategies. When it comes to commercial real estate, understanding how to effectively plan and execute an exit can make the difference between average and exceptional gains. Whether you're a seasoned investor or a newcomer aiming to diversify your portfolio, grasping the nuances of various exit strategies is crucial for optimizing your investment outcomes.

One common challenge investors face is the complexity involved in exiting commercial real estate investments. Unlike the simplicity of selling stocks or bonds, real estate transactions come with numerous considerations – from market conditions and tax implications to legal requirements and financial commitments. For instance, while a sale-leaseback arrangement might offer immediate liquidity, it demands thorough scrutiny of lease terms to avoid unfavorable long-term obligations. Similarly, leveraging 1031 exchanges to defer capital gains taxes requires meticulous planning and compliance with strict IRS timelines. These intricacies highlight the importance of not only knowing your options but also understanding how each strategy aligns with your broader investment goals.

  In this chapter, we delve into two prominent exit strategies tailored for commercial real estate: sale-leaseback arrangements and 1031 exchanges. You'll gain insights into how sale-leasebacks can provide liquidity without sacrificing operational control and learn about the critical aspects to consider when structuring such deals. Additionally, we will explore the mechanics of 1031 exchanges, focusing on their benefits, requirements, and the strategic foresight needed to execute them successfully. By the end of this chapter, you will be equipped with practical knowledge and actionable steps to implement these exit strategies, ensuring that your commercial real estate investments yield optimal returns while aligning with your financial objectives.

Leveraging Sale-Leaseback Arrangements for Liquidity

To explore the option of sale-leaseback arrangements for achieving cash liquidity after investing in commercial properties, we first need to understand what a sale-leaseback entails. In its simplest form, a sale-leaseback is an agreement where you sell your property to a buyer and then lease it back from them. This allows you to convert the equity tied up in the property into liquid capital that can be used for other investments or operational needs. By doing so, you don't lose operational control of the property, keeping the day-to-day business unaffected.

For the investors, this is particularly advantageous as it provides immediate access to funds without having to uproot operations or disrupt the flow of business. It's almost like refinancing your property but with the added benefit of removing ownership burdens such as maintenance costs and property taxes. However, understanding the terms of the lease agreement is crucial because they will dictate your financial and operational commitments moving forward.

When examining the terms of a lease agreement, one must meticulously review the duration, rental rates, and any clauses related to potential buyback options. These details are pivotal for ensuring that you're not locking yourself into a situation that becomes financially untenable down the line. For instance, be wary of escalation clauses that cause rent to increase at unsustainable rates over time. Review the termination clauses to know what happens if either party decides to end the lease prematurely. Also, it's worth considering whether there is an option to repurchase the property at some point in the future.

Here is what you can do in order to achieve the goal:

- Begin by thoroughly reviewing the sale-leaseback agreement, paying attention to all financial terms.
- Negotiate terms that align with your long-term financial goals and ensure sustainability.
- Seek professional advice from a real estate attorney or financial advisor to understand the fine print and implications fully.
- Consider the stability and reliability of the buyer to safeguard against the risk of default on their part.
- Plan for contingencies by evaluating alternative funding sources or operational strategies should the lease terms become unfavorable.

Once you've understood and agreed upon the lease's terms, another critical aspect is proper financial planning. This should involve assessing both the immediate influx of capital and the long-term financial implications. While the immediate cash boost can be highly beneficial, it's vital to ensure that the lease payments don't adversely affect your overall cash flow in the years to come.

In financial planning, consider creating a detailed budget that outlines how the incoming capital will be allocated. Whether it's for expanding your business, paying down high-interest debt, or making new investments, having a clear plan mitigates the risk of misallocating these newfound resources. Additionally, employ scenario analysis to predict how different economic conditions might affect your ability to meet lease obligations. This includes considering worst-case scenarios where market conditions could turn unfavorable.

Proper assessment cannot be overstated. Before you even embark on a sale-leaseback arrangement, simulate various financial outcomes based on different lease durations and rental rates. Use historical data and market trends to inform these models. The aim is to be well-prepared for potential financial strains that might arise from fluctuating market conditions.

Another significant consideration is the long-term implications of this strategy. It's easy to get caught up in the allure of immediate liquidity, but remember that you are essentially trading ownership for operational control. This can have lasting impacts on your balance sheet and financial health. Analyzing long-term implications involves looking beyond the immediate benefits to evaluate how this decision aligns with your overall investment strategy and future objectives.

Balance is key here. The primary advantage of a sale-leaseback is achieving liquidity without losing operational continuity. This means you can continue running your business effectively while using the released capital to fuel growth or stabilize finances. However, the flip side is the ongoing obligation to make regular lease payments, which introduces a new layer of financial commitment. Hence, weigh these aspects carefully to make sure the benefits outweigh the drawbacks.

Ultimately, sale-leaseback arrangements offer a compelling balance between liquidity and operational continuity, making them a viable exit strategy for real estate investments. They provide a pathway to unlock the value tied up in your property, offering flexibility and financial freedom. Just remember, the essence lies in meticulous planning, thorough assessment, and smart financial management to maximize the benefits while safeguarding against potential risks.

We've covered quite a bit on sale-leasebacks, but let's pause and think about how aligning this approach with empirical evidence can further solidify its effectiveness. Case studies and data points underline how businesses have successfully leveraged this strategy. Likewise, staying informed through market research and evolving real estate trends can help in making data-driven decisions that enhance profitability and ensure sustainability.

At the core, we should always prioritize human welfare and practical sustainability over mere economic growth. A well-planned sale-leaseback arrangement achieves this by providing the necessary financial tools while ensuring operational stability. This nuanced approach not only maximizes returns but does so responsibly, balancing personal responsibility with the need for a collective safety net.

The sale-leaseback strategy, therefore, is not merely about transactional efficiency but also about cultivating a more resilient, adaptable investment portfolio. By emphasizing empirical data and sound financial principles, we create pathways for intelligent, thoughtful wealth expansion, reflective of a responsible stewardship of one's assets. Through careful planning and execution, a sale-leaseback can indeed serve as a prudent, efficacious method for enhancing liquidity within the commercial real estate investment landscape.

Maximizing Tax Efficiency with 1031 Exchanges

Planning Effective Exit Strategies for Optimal Returns on Commercial Real Estate Investments

One powerful method to optimize and expand your real estate portfolio while deferring significant tax obligations is through 1031 exchanges. This IRS code provision allows investors to sell a property and reinvest the proceeds into a "like-kind" property, thus deferring capital gains taxes. Essentially, it enables you to trade up, diversify, or consolidate your holdings without the immediate concern of a hefty tax bill, paving a smoother path for portfolio growth.

Understanding the ins and outs of 1031 exchanges begins with recognizing their core benefits. By deferring capital gains taxes, you can utilize the full amount of your sale proceeds to invest in the new property. This means more capital at your disposal, allowing you to aim for higher-value properties or diversify across different types of commercial real estates, such as from office spaces to retail centers or industrial warehouses. The power here lies in compounding returns, where your portfolio can grow exponentially over time given the larger base you're working with.

However, executing a successful 1031 exchange involves navigating several strict timelines and requirements. There are key deadlines you must adhere to, such as identifying potential replacement properties within 45 days from the sale of your original property. Additionally, the exchange must be completed within 180 days. Missing these windows could result in disqualification of the tax deferment, leading to an unexpected tax liability. Thus, it's essential to plan meticulously, often engaging a Qualified Intermediary to facilitate the process and ensure compliance with regulations.

Here is what you can do in order to achieve the goal:

- First, identify and engage a Qualified Intermediary early in your planning process.
- Then, keep detailed records and closely monitor the timeline to avoid any lapses.
- Next, promptly identify replacement properties and document them within the 45-day window.
- Finally, complete the purchase and transfer of the new property within the 180 days stipulated by IRS rules.

The importance of properly identifying suitable replacement properties cannot be overstated. Your chosen replacements should align not only with the like-kind requirement but also with your investment goals. For instance, if aiming for higher cash flow, you might consider properties with higher rental yields. Conversely, for long-term appreciation, look at properties in emerging markets with robust economic indicators. Conducting thorough due diligence on these potential investments is crucial to avoid pitfalls that can erode your returns.

Additionally, due diligence extends beyond just financial metrics. Understanding the local market dynamics, future development plans, zoning laws, and tenant stability contribute significantly to assessing a property's potential. It's about assembling a broader picture where each piece of information helps mitigate risks and maximize rewards.

Here is what you can do in order to achieve the goal:
- Start by researching market trends and future economic developments in the area.
- Evaluate the physical condition and maintenance history of the property to anticipate any future repairs or upgrades needed.
- Review the lease agreements and tenant profiles to assess reliability and consistency of income.
- Lastly, consult with legal and tax advisors to understand the implications of the transaction fully.

Strategically utilizing 1031 exchanges goes hand in hand with managing your real estate holdings for optimized returns. Consider how holding periods impact your overall strategy. Shorter holding periods may allow quicker portfolio turnover, facilitating faster access to capital gains and reinvestments. However, longer holding periods might provide steadier cash flows and potential appreciation over time. It's essential to strike a balance that reflects both your current financial needs and long-term investment goals.

Balancing economic growth with human welfare is crucial, particularly when considering the implications of commercial real estate investments on communities. Thoughtful development and management practices can lead to sustainable growth benefiting investors and residents alike. This includes integrating green building initiatives, fostering inclusive community engagement, and ensuring affordable commercial spaces that support small businesses. These actions not only enhance social responsibility but can also improve property desirability and value proposition in the marketplace.

Personal responsibility intertwined with a safety net approach underscores the need for preparedness against unforeseen challenges. The commercial real estate market, like any other, is subject to volatility and economic shifts. Having a robust contingency plan can cushion against downturns. Diversification, maintaining adequate reserves, and staying informed about market cycles can act as a safety net during turbulent times.

In conclusion, planning effective exit strategies using 1031 exchanges requires a blend of strategic foresight, adherence to regulatory timelines, diligent property identification, and a balanced approach to economic and societal impacts. It's about leveraging empirical evidence and data-driven insights to make informed decisions that drive both individual wealth and broader community well-being.

Strategic Exits: Unlocking Value and Mitigating Risk

Throughout this chapter, we delved into the strategic use of sale-leaseback arrangements and 1031 exchanges as effective exit strategies for optimizing returns on commercial real estate investments. By understanding these mechanisms and applying them prudently, investors can unlock significant value tied up in their properties while maintaining operational control.

Returning to our initial discussion, the primary intention behind leveraging sale-leasebacks is to achieve liquidity without compromising business stability. This approach enables access to capital that would otherwise remain immobilized in property holdings. It's a way to secure immediate cash flow to fuel growth, pay down debts, or diversify one's investment portfolio. However, careful consideration of lease terms and financial planning remains paramount to ensure long-term viability.

On the other hand, 1031 exchanges offer a powerful tool to defer capital gains taxes, thereby maximizing the reinvestment potential within your real estate portfolio. This strategy allows you to grow your investments exponentially by using deferred tax funds to acquire higher-value properties or diversify into different commercial sectors. Yet, it necessitates meticulous adherence to regulatory timelines and thorough due diligence in identifying suitable replacement properties.

Readers should be mindful of several concerns when implementing these strategies. The ramifications of locking into unfavorable lease terms or failing to comply with 1031 exchange deadlines could lead to substantial financial strain or unexpected tax liabilities. Moreover, the intricate nature of these transactions warrants professional guidance to navigate potential pitfalls properly.

In a broader sense, these strategies have significant implications. They not only bolster individual wealth but also contribute to overall economic vitality. Thoughtfully managed commercial properties can lead to sustainable community development, fostering environments that support local businesses and enhance urban resilience.

As we conclude this exploration of sale-leasebacks and 1031 exchanges, it's essential to reflect on the delicate balance between achieving financial objectives and maintaining ethical stewardship of assets. Properly executed, these methods can serve as prudent pathways to enhance liquidity and invest wisely within the commercial real estate landscape.

Looking ahead, continued research and adaptive strategies rooted in empirical evidence will be crucial for navigating the evolving market dynamics. In this journey of wealth expansion, never lose sight of the broader impacts, embracing practices that generate both individual prosperity and collective well-being.

www.ingramcontent.com/pod-product-compliance
Lightning Source LLC
Chambersburg PA
CBHW071458220526
45472CB00003B/847